Bible Facts Recitation

for kids

Bible Facts Recitation

for kids

Book One: Creation & Covenant

Genesis – Deuteronomy

Caroline Weerstra

Catechism for Kids

Visit our website:
www.catechismforkids.com

Published by Common Life Press, Schenectady, New York. 2017.

ISBN-13: 978-0-9898143-9-3

All Bible verses quoted in this workbook are from the New King James (NKJV) translation unless otherwise specified.

Introduction

OUR PURPOSE

When my daughter Sydney began reading the Bible on her own at age six, she had many questions:

"Mom, was King Saul the same Saul on the road to Damascus?"

"Which came first: the big flood or the ten plagues?"

"Did Peter or Paul write any of the psalms?"

It soon became clear that although my daughter had learned many Bible stories and psalms, she lacked a basic framework in which to understand them. The sheer number of names (some of which are duplicates) and the vast expanse of time covered in the whole of Scripture can be overwhelming.

This difficulty must have been obvious to the men who organized the sixty-six books of the Bible into the order we see in most versions of Scripture today. Great attention was payed to properly categorizing the books and setting them in a chronological sequence whenever possible, so readers could grasp the flow of the story and appreciate the variety of literature (history, law, psalms, and so on).

Yet for young children who merely learn selections of stories and memory verses in Sunday school, the framework of Scripture as a whole is not obvious.

We have designed this curriculum specifically to address this gap in Bible comprehension. While our curriculum does not delve deeply into particular Bible stories, it presents an overall picture and some basic Bible facts designed to assist children in absorbing and categorizing the story of redemption from Genesis to Revelation.

This first book in the *Bible Facts Recitation* series covers the Bible from Genesis through Deuteronomy in five chapters. Each chapter contains an explanation of important events and concepts, a list of characters and themes, catechism questions and answers, and a rhyme to help children remember important ideas. Additional information may include lists, maps, or family trees. We place particular emphasis on major events, important characters, and chronological progression.

TEACHING BIBLE FACTS

Children love to memorize! And most children find memorization relatively easy. As a parent or teacher, feel free to encourage your students to recite even large quantities of information (the books of the Bible, the days of creation, the tribes of Israel, and so on) from memory. Remember that you are helping them build a foundation with which they can better understand the entirety of Scripture.

Begin each chapter in this book with the reading portion so that your students understand the purpose of the material. As you progress through each reading section, ask the corresponding catechism questions for that portion of material and help the children respond with the correct answers. If you have time, you may teach students to memorize the catechism answers, but most teachers allow children to respond with an approximate summary, not word-for-word recitation. For example, a child responding to the question, "What is the Bible?" with the answer, "The Bible is the Word of God, and it tells us how to honor and obey God" has given a correct response, even though it is not exactly phrased as the catechism answer. It is strongly advised that you do NOT skip the question-and-answer phase of learning, since it establishes that your students truly understand the information presented.

Consider the goals provided at the beginning of each chapter and make sure they are met with the resources that follow the reading and catechism sections. For example, one goal of the first chapter is that your students learn the books of the Bible. You may choose to have the children recite the books of the Bible in order, or you may choose to help them memorize the Books of the Bible Rhyme. Either method will achieve the goal of memorization of the books of the Bible. Choose the method that works best for your particular class and age level.

Make learning fun! Rhythm and rhyme often help children (and adults!) remember information more easily. Hand motions also help retain information while giving children an opportunity to move around and use up some energy! Competitions with small rewards (candy or prizes) motivate classes to work hard. Be creative in your use of the resources provided in this book.

The speed at which you move through the curriculum depends on your schedule and your particular goals for the class. It is generally recommended that you spend at least three weeks working through each chapter so that students will have adequate time to absorb and memorize the basic recitations included in the chapter.

As you move on to the next chapter, you should review before each lesson by reciting some of the material from previous chapters so that your students do not forget what they have learned. For example, when you reach the last chapter of this book, you may begin the lesson by having your class recite the books of the Bible, the days of creation, and the tribes of Israel before moving on to your lesson for the day. This ensures that students practice and perfect their memorization of important information even as they continue to add to their repertoire of recitation.

CHILDREN WITH DISABILITIES

Even as you encourage students to memorize, be aware that some children are less capable of retaining information than others. Children who struggle with learning disabilities often become discouraged and give up trying to learn, since they are constantly behind everyone else.

If you find that a particular child in your class is having trouble keeping up with the rest of the group, consider ways to include the child. Here are a few suggestions:

- **Set up teams for competitions, pairing a strong learner with a weak learner on the same team.** Do not allow teams to self-select or the child with learning disabilities will constantly undergo the embarrassment of being chosen last.

- **Use a highlighter to mark challenging questions in your notes.** Ask simple questions of students who struggle more, and save challenging questions for students who enjoy a challenge.

- **Always recite TOGETHER (books of the Bible, memory verses, and so on) as a group.** This allows children with disabilities to keep up with the class by listening to their classmates.

- **Above all, do not permit anyone in the class to mock or humiliate a slow learner.**

Remember: the purpose of Bible Facts Recitation is to encourage ALL students to study and understand the Bible. It is not a survival game in which only the strong prevail. Do your best to ensure that disabled children are able to gain something from the class, even though they may not learn as rapidly as other students.

PRAY

Parents and Sunday school teachers often feel that their work is dismissed by others as unimportant in the overall function of the church. But the children you teach today are the fathers, mothers, pastors, teachers, and mission workers of the future. Teaching children is crucial work, and you need to pray often!

Ask God to grant you wisdom and skill in serving His children. Pray for any difficulties you encounter while teaching. Ask that God would open the hearts and minds of your students to His Word so that they may know God and serve Him through the rest of their days and into eternity.

Caroline Weerstra
Catechism for Kids

Part 1

The Bible

You should know...

- the books of the Bible
- how the Bible is organized

The law of the LORD is perfect, converting the soul;
The testimony of the LORD is sure, making wise the simple;
The statutes of the LORD are right, rejoicing the heart;
The commandment of the LORD is pure, enlightening the eyes;
The fear of the LORD is clean, enduring forever;
The judgments of the LORD are true and righteous altogether.
More to be desired are they than gold,
Yea, than much fine gold;
Sweeter also than honey and the honeycomb.
Moreover by them Your servant is warned,
And in keeping them there is great reward.

- Psalm 19:7-11

The Bible

THE WORD OF GOD

All Scripture is given by inspiration of God, and is profitable for doctrine, for reproof, for correction, for instruction in righteousness, that the man of God may be complete, thoroughly equipped for every good work.   –II Timothy 3:16-17

The Bible (also called **Scripture**) is God's message to us. It tells us who God is and what we should do to honor and obey Him.

Take a moment to look around. If you are sitting in your house or in a classroom, perhaps you can see the sky through the window. Maybe you can see the sun shining or the stars twinkling. Look down at your hands. Think about how each finger is made up of bones and muscles that respond to whatever you want to do (pick up a pencil, tie your shoes, or shake hands with a friend). Now listen—do you hear yourself breathing the air that God has provided for you? Can you hear the wind outside rustling through leaves?

The apostle Paul wrote that we can learn much about God simply by looking around at various things God has made: "For since the creation of the world, His invisible attributes are clearly seen, being understood by the things that are made" (Romans 1:20). Just by looking around, we should realize that God is wise and that He is kind. We can see that He is powerful since He made all these things, and we can see that He cares about His creatures because He provides so tenderly for us.

However, because we are foolish and sinful creatures, we can never see clearly enough to gain a proper understanding of God just by looking around at the world. Unless God reveals Himself to us more plainly, we have no hope of truly knowing Him. God provides for those He loves in every way—not only by giving us food, water, friends, and family—but also by giving us a way to know Him.

The Bible supplies everything we need to know about God—who He is and how we should obey Him. It is our instruction manual that (as Paul said to Timothy) equips us for every good work (II Timothy 3:17). We should receive God's Word with love and thankfulness. We should read it often, praying that God will help us understand it and apply it to our lives.

HOW THE BIBLE IS ORGANIZED

Now, therefore, you are no longer strangers and foreigners, but fellow citizens with the saints and members of the household of God, having been built on the foundation of the apostles and prophets, Jesus Christ Himself being the chief cornerstone. –Ephesians 2:19-20

The Bible was written by people who were specifically chosen by God and taught what to say by the Holy Spirit. These writers fall into two basic categories: **prophets** (who received revelation from God through visions or prophecies) and **apostles** (who were chosen by God as eye-witnesses of Christ's ministry, death, and resurrection).

The Bible is not a single book composed by one author. It is actually more like a library of small books written by different prophets and apostles. In fact, there are sixty-six different books all collected together as the **canon of Scripture**. These books contain all kinds of writing. Some books (like I & II Chronicles) are history books telling us stories about God's people. Other books (like Psalms) are songbooks teaching us to sing praise to God. We have writings of prophets like Ezekiel and Hosea foretelling future events and calling people to repent. We have records of Jesus' ministry written by His disciples. Finally, we have letters sent by early church leaders to various churches and individuals instructing them on Christian life and doctrine.

This vast array of information needs to be carefully organized so that readers can understand. The main categories of the Bible are very simple. All writings from before the time of Christ are called the **Old Testament**. All writings from after the time of Christ are called the **New Testament**.

However, since there are so many different types of books, the Bible needs further organization than these two big sections. Both parts contains sub-categories of books.

The Old Testament is organized into these categories:

1. **Books of Moses** (also called the **Pentateuch**): the first five books of the Bible, including history of the creation of the world, God's covenant, and the law.

2. **Historical Books**: stories about God's people through the Old Testament era, from the time God established His people as a nation in the Promised Land to the time He sent them into exile for their sins.

3. **Devotional Books** (also called **Wisdom Books**): songs and wise sayings to help us worship and obey God.

4. **Major Prophets**: long books written by Old Testament prophets.

5. **Minor Prophets**: short books written by Old Testament prophets.

The New Testament is organized into these categories:

1. **The Gospels**: records of the life, ministry, teaching, death, and resurrection of Jesus.

2. **History Book**: the book of Acts, containing history of the earliest Christians – from the ascension of Jesus to the imprisonment of the apostle Paul.

3. **Pauline Epistles**: letters written by the apostle Paul to early Christians.

4. **Other Epistles**: letters written by other apostles and church leaders to early Christians.

5. **Apocalyptic** (also called **Prophecy**) **Book**: the prophetic visions of the apostle John in the book of Revelation.

Catechism on the Bible

Q1. What is the Bible?

A.   The Bible is a collection of writings through which God reveals to us who He is and what we must do to honor and obey Him.   We refer to the Bible also as the **Word of God** or the **Scriptures.**

Q2. Who wrote the Bible?

A.   The Bible was written by people who were specifically chosen by God and taught what to say by the Holy Spirit.

Q3. How many books are in the Bible?

A.   The Bible contains sixty-six books.

Q4. What are the two main parts of the Bible?

A.   The two main parts of the Bible are the Old Testament and the New Testament.

Q5. How is the Old Testament organized?

A.   The Old Testament is organized into five parts – Books of Moses, Historical Books, Devotional Books, Major Prophets, and Minor Prophets.

Q6. In which language was the Old Testament written?

A.   The Old Testament was written in Hebrew, the language of God's chosen people.

Q7. How is the New Testament organized?

A.   The New Testament is organized into five parts – Gospels, History Book, Pauline Epistles, Other Epistles, and Apocalyptic Book.

Q8. **In which language was the New Testament written?**

    A.   The New Testament was written in Greek, which was the most common language in the world at the time of its writing.

Q9. **Is the Bible complete?**

    A.   Yes, the Bible is complete. Nothing may be added to the Bible or taken away from the Bible.

Q10. **How should we read the Bible?**

    A.   We should read the Bible often and with reverence. We should pray about what we learn and consider how to apply God's Word to our lives.

Books of the Old Testament

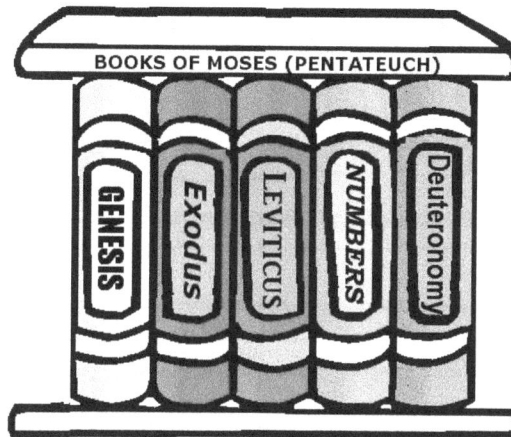

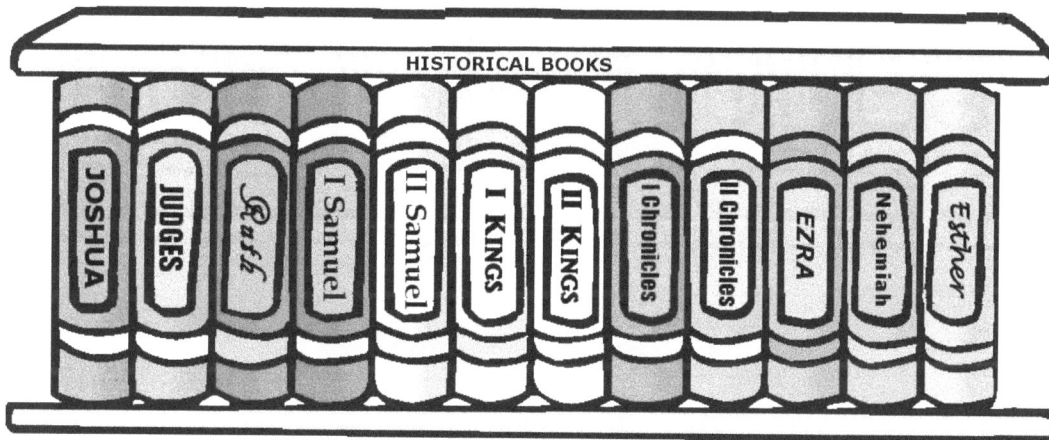

BOOKS OF MOSES (PENTATEUCH)

GENESIS · Exodus · LEVITICUS · NUMBERS · Deuteronomy

HISTORICAL BOOKS

JOSHUA · JUDGES · Ruth · I Samuel · II Samuel · I KINGS · II KINGS · I Chronicles · II Chronicles · EZRA · Nehemiah · Esther

DEVOTIONAL (WISDOM) BOOKS

JOB · Psalms · Proverbs · Ecclesiastes · SONG OF SOLOMON

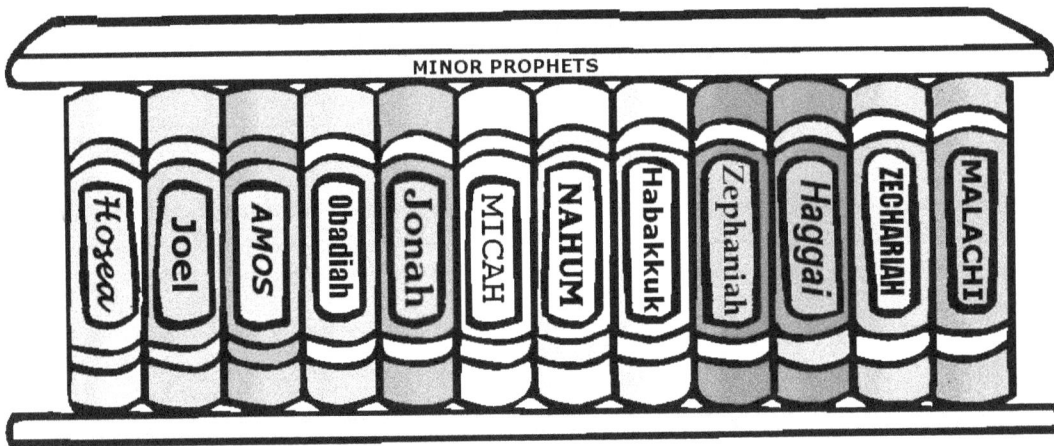

Books of the New Testament

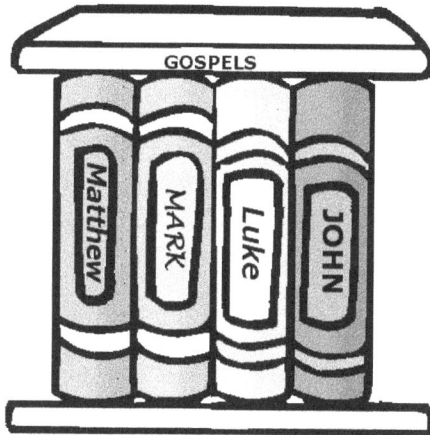

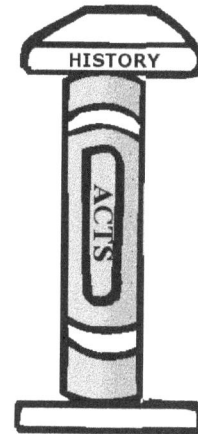

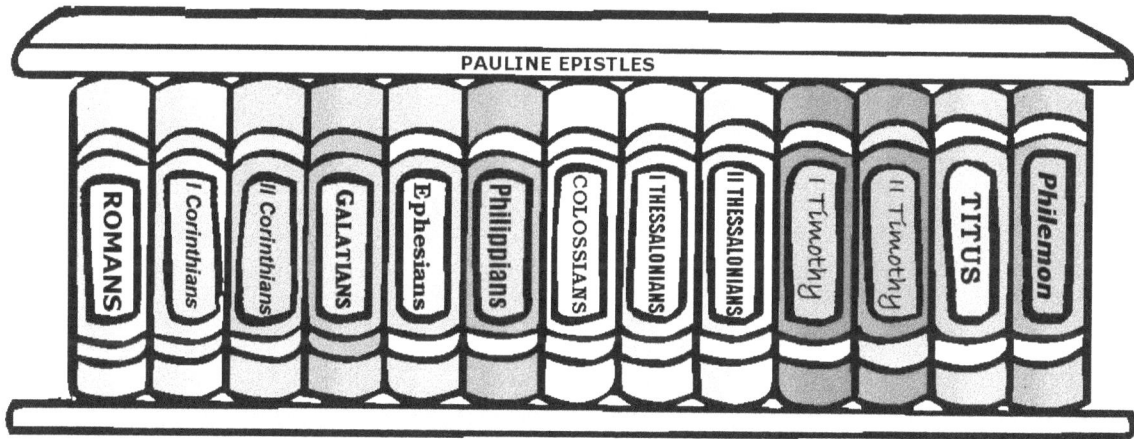

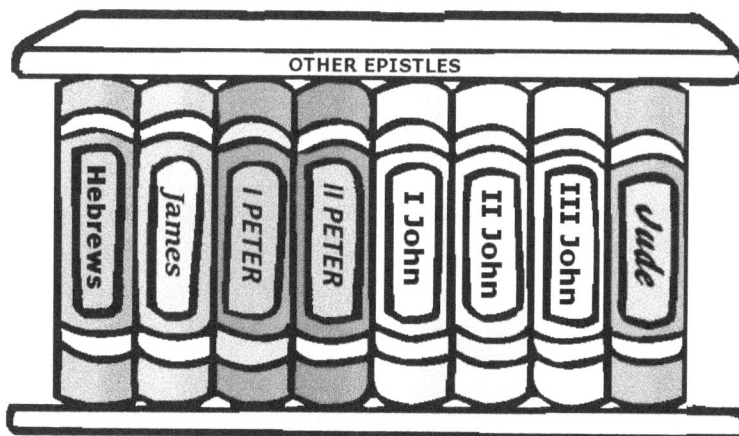

GOSPELS

Matthew | MARK | Luke | JOHN

HISTORY

ACTS

PAULINE EPISTLES

ROMANS | I Corinthians | II Corinthians | GALATIANS | Ephesians | Philippians | COLOSSIANS | I THESSALONIANS | II THESSALONIANS | I Timothy | II Timothy | TITUS | Philemon

OTHER EPISTLES

Hebrews | James | I PETER | II PETER | I John | II John | III John | Jude

APOCALYPTIC

REVELATION

(PROPHECY)

Books of the Bible Chart

OLD TESTAMENT	
BOOKS OF MOSES (PENTATEUCH)	
GENESIS	The book of beginnings: creation, the fall, and God's promise of a Redeemer. God establishes His covenant with Abraham and his descendants.
EXODUS	After establishing Moses as leader of His people, God rescues His people from bondage in Egypt. He once again makes a covenant with them in the giving of the Law, and He provides a Tabernacle to dwell with His people.
LEVITICUS	God's people must be holy as He is holy, and so they are required to keep His commands regarding purity and to sacrifice for atonement for their sins.
NUMBERS	God graciously provides for His people, but they constantly rebel against Him. When given the opportunity to take possession of the Promised Land, Israel's faith falters.
DEUTERONOMY	Moses delivers his farewell sermon to the people of Israel as they come again to the threshold of the Promised Land. Moses cannot enter the land because of his disobedience, but he urges Israel to walk in the way of life.
HISTORICAL BOOKS	
JOSHUA	Joshua leads the Israelites into Canaan and takes possession of the land.
JUDGES	The people of Israel continually fall into sin, for which God judges them. When they call out to God, He provides judges to lead them.
RUTH	Boaz serves as kinsman-redeemer for Ruth—providing for her and eventually marrying her. This book serves as background for the rise of King David.
I SAMUEL	Samuel is Israel's judge, but the people ask for a king. God provides them with Saul. Saul is unfaithful toward God, and so God anoints David as the next king of Israel.
II SAMUEL	David becomes king of Israel, but he sins against God. God judges David and his descendants for those sins.

I KINGS	Solomon ascends to the throne and builds the Temple. Israel departs from God and is judged. The kingdom is divided when Jereboam and the northern tribes break away from Solomon's son Rehoboam.
II KINGS	Israel's people are unfaithful toward God. They are conquered by Assyria because of their sins. Some of Judah's kings are faithful, but disobedience eventually leads to exile in Babylon.
I CHRONICLES & II CHRONICLES	Much of the history in these books overlaps I & II Kings. However Chronicles encourages the Jews in exile by reviewing their heritage and reminding them to trust in the promises of God.
EZRA	The Jews return from exile. In spite of much opposition, they rebuild the Temple.
NEHEMIAH	Under the leadership of Nehemiah and Ezra, Judah rebuilds the defense wall around Jerusalem.
ESTHER	During the exile in Babylon, Haman devises a plot to kill all the race of Mordecai. Through the faithfulness of Esther and the providence of God, the Jews are saved.
DEVOTIONAL BOOKS (WISDOM BOOKS)	
JOB	Job is righteous and yet he suffers. He learns to trust God even in times of great trouble. God knows all things and works them out for His glory.
PSALMS	This book of songs provides a window into the heart and many emotions of the righteous in a fallen world.
PROVERBS	The proverbs are brief, practical statements which provide wisdom for life.
ECCLESIASTES	The search for meaning and joy must begin with the fear of the Lord and keeping His commandments. Life without God is meaningless.
SONG OF SOLOMON	Also called *Song of Songs*, this book teaches about marital love which reflects the love that Christ has for the Church.
MAJOR PROPHETS	
ISAIAH	God will judge His people for their sins and their stubborn refusal to submit to Him. However He will comfort His people when He restores them to Himself. Isaiah emphasizes the work of the coming Messiah.
JEREMIAH	Jeremiah brings a message of doom to Judah and warns about the coming disaster from Babylon.

LAMENTATIONS	Probably composed by Jeremiah, this book laments the judgment of God on His people, but speaks also of hope in God's mercy.
EZEKIEL	Is God unfair to Judah? Ezekiel defends God's judgment against His disobedient people. The glory of the Lord departs from the Temple, but Ezekiel foretells restoration.
DANIEL	Daniel and his friends serve God even in exile. This book speaks of the sovereignty of God and how He uses the kingdoms of this world to bring about the everlasting kingdom of Christ.
MINOR PROPHETS	
HOSEA	The people of Israel are worshiping pagan gods. God compares Israel to an unfaithful wife who has broken the covenant.
JOEL	God has sent disaster on Judah in the form of a locust plague on the crops. Joel declares that Judah must repent.
AMOS	In Israel, the wealthy are increasing riches at the expense of the poor. Amos prophesies the Day of the Lord in which God will judge the sins of Israel.
OBADIAH	When enemies attack Judah, nearby Edom helps loot and destroy Jerusalem. Obadiah prophesies that God will punish those who give aid to the enemies of His people.
JONAH	God commands Jonah to warn Nineveh about coming judgment. Jonah refuses to go, and God causes him to be swallowed by a fish for three days. Later Jonah preaches to Nineveh; the city repents.
MICAH	Micah declares God's judgement on Samaria and Judah because of their idolatry and corruption. But this prophet also foretells the rebuilding of Zion and the coming of the Messiah.
NAHUM	Nineveh has caused much suffering, and God will bring about justice in the destruction of the city.
HABAKKUK	Habakkuk cries out the Lord because of the violence and corruption around him. God is bringing about justice through the Chaldeans, but this also is a calamity. Habakkuk declares that he will rejoice in the Lord no matter the circumstances.
ZEPHANIAH	Judgment is coming on Judah on the Day of the Lord, but God will spare a remnant to restore His people.
HAGGAI	Work on rebuilding of the Temple is languishing. God's people are called to be zealous for God and to devote themselves to building up the Temple.

ZECHARIAH	The visions of Zechariah bring comfort to the remnant of Judah. The prophet foretells the kingdom of the Messiah that will extend over the whole earth.
MALACHI	God's people complain that He has neglected them, but Malachi reminds them of their own unfaithfulness in serving God.

NEW TESTAMENT

GOSPELS

MATTHEW	This gospel tells about the life, death, and resurrection of Jesus with special emphasis on His sovereignty. Christ is the Messiah, the fulfillment of Old Testament prophecies.
MARK	Mark's account of the life, death, and resurrection of Jesus focuses on His humility – that He came to give His life for His people.
LUKE	The gospel of Luke presents the good news of Jesus to a Gentile audience, proclaiming Him as the hope of the whole world.
JOHN	John emphasizes the deity of Christ as he tells the story of Jesus' life, death, and resurrection. He declares plainly that Jesus is the same God who created all things.

HISTORY

ACTS	After Jesus ascends, the Holy Spirit enables the gospel to thrive and spread among new believers. Paul and his companions bring the good news of Christ to the Gentiles.

PAULINE EPISTLES

ROMANS	Gentiles and Jews have all broken God's commands. Salvation is only found through faith in Christ. Believers are united to Christ and no longer bound to sin.
I CORINTHIANS	Division and immorality trouble the church in Corinth. Paul urges Corinthian believers to be united in Christ and to live holy lives imitating Christ.
II CORINTHIANS	Paul responds to those who try to discredit his ministry, and he urges the Corinthians toward forgiveness, wisdom, and generosity.
GALATIANS	The law of Moses points us toward Christ, but salvation is found in Christ alone. Gentile and Jewish believers are united in Christ.

EPHESIANS	God's people have been chosen for salvation. Salvation is by grace, but all Christians should live in a manner worthy of their calling in Christ.
PHILIPPIANS	From prison, Paul writes to urge the church at Philippi to rejoice in the Lord and to live humbly as Christ did.
COLOSSIANS	Paul opposes false teachers who have misled the church at Colossi. He declares the supremacy of Christ and urges the Colossians toward faith and obedience.
I THESSALONIANS	The church at Thessalonica is encouraged toward greater maturity in Christ—especially purity, orderly living, and hope in the resurrection.
II THESSALONIANS	Paul encourages the Thessalonians in their difficulties, assuring them of the certainty of Christ's return.
I TIMOTHY	Timothy receives instructions about the organization and administration of churches.
II TIMOTHY	Paul urges Timothy to be bold and unwavering in the face of persecution.
TITUS	This epistles gives details about qualification for leadership in the church and the qualities of proper Christian society.
PHILEMON	Paul writes a personal letter to Philemon on behalf of a runaway slave Onesimus. Since Onesimus and Philemon have both declared faith in Christ, Paul urges the former slave-owner to accept Onesimus as a brother.
GENERAL EPISTLES	
HEBREWS	Hebrews presents Christ as both Priest and the sacrifice for sin. We are urged to persevere in faith even through great trials.
JAMES	Written in the style of wisdom literature, this epistle urges practical faith that finds expression in good works and self-control.
I PETER	Peter calls believers to live in holiness and to face persecution with rejoicing. Elders are challenged to faithful shepherding of God's people.
II PETER	This epistle warns against false teacher and urges the faithful to prepare themselves for the Day of the Lord.
I JOHN	John declares that God loves His people, and so all who are faithful must love each other and live in holiness.

II JOHN	Loving God means obeying His commands. John warns against false teachers and urges diligent discernment.
III JOHN	True believers are known by their actions. Those who do evil are not from God. God's people must imitate good.
JUDE	This epistle warns against false teachers and calls believers to persevere in faith.
APOCALYPTIC (PROPHECY)	
REVELATION	John delivers messages from Christ to the churches along with prophetic visions.

Books of the Bible Rhyme

OLD TESTAMENT

In **Genesis** the world was made,
In **Exodus** the march is told;
Leviticus contains the law;
In **Numbers** are the tribes enrolled.

In **Deuteronomy** again
We're urged to keep God's law alone;
And these five Books of Moses make
The oldest holy writing known.

•   •   •   •   •

Brave **Joshua** to Canaan leads;
In **Judges** oft the Jews rebel;
We read of David's name in **Ruth**
And **First and Second Samuel**.

In **First and Second Kings**, we read
How bad the Hebrew state became;
In **First and Second Chronicles**
Another history of the same.

In **Ezra** captive Jews return,
While **Nehemiah** builds the wall;
Queen **Esther** saves her race from death –
These books 'Historical' we call.

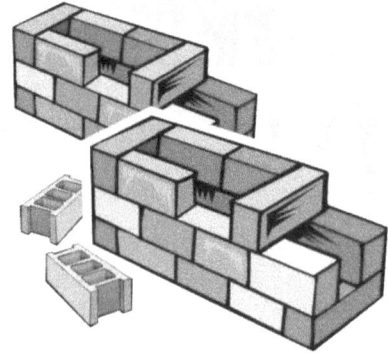

• • • •

In **Job** we read of patient faith;
In **Psalms** are David's songs of praise;
The **Proverbs** are to make us wise;
Ecclesiastes next portrays

How fleeting earthly pleasures are;
The **Song of Solomon** is all
About true love like Christ's –
And these five books 'Devotional' we call.

• • • •

Isaiah tells of Christ to come;
While **Jeremiah** tells of woe,
And in his **Lamentations** mourns
The holy city's overthrow.

Ezekiel speaks of mysteries,
And **Daniel** foretells kings of old;
Hosea over Israel grieves;
In **Joel** blessings are foretold.

24

In **Amos** too are Israel's woes,
And **Obadiah**'s sent to warn,
While **Jonah** shows that Christ should die,
And **Micah** where He should be born.

In **Nahum** Nineveh is seen;
Habakkuk tells of Chaldea's guilt;
In **Zephaniah** are Judah's sins;
In **Haggai**, the Temple's built.

Then **Zechariah** speaks of Christ,
And **Malachi** His sign;
The Prophets number seventeen,
And all the books are thirty-nine.

•　•　•　•　•

NEW TESTAMENT

Matthew, **Mark**, **Luke**, and **John**
Tell what Christ did in every place.
The **Acts** tell what the apostles did,
And **Romans** how we're saved by grace.

Corinthians instructs the church;
Galatians shows us faith alone,
Ephesians true love, and in
Philippians, God's grace is shown.

Colossians tells us more of Christ
And **Thessalonians** of the end;
In **Timothy** and **Titus** both
Are rules for pastors to attend.

Philemon Christian friendship shows,
Then **Hebrews** clearly tells how all
The Jewish law prefigured Christ –
Most epistles are by Paul.

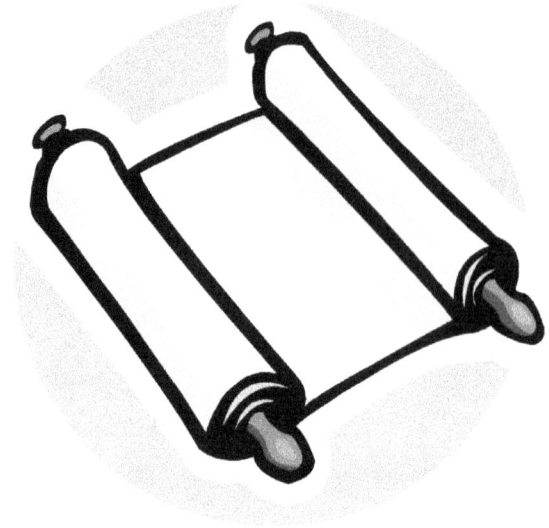

James shows that faith by works
must live,
And **Peter** urges steadfastness,
While **John** exhorts to Christian love,
For those who have it God will bless.

Jude shows the end of evil men;
Revelation tells of heaven.
This ends the whole New Testament –
All the books are twenty-seven.

Part 2

Beginnings

Genesis 1 – 11

You should know...

- the days of Creation
- basic facts and major characters involved in:
  - Creation & the Fall
  - the Flood
  - the Tower of Babel

When I consider Your heavens, the work of Your fingers,
The moon and the stars, which You have ordained,
What is man that You are mindful of him,
And the son of man that You visit him?
For You have made him a little lower than the angels,
And You have crowned him with glory and honor.

- Psalm 8:3-5

Characters and Themes

Major Characters from Genesis 1-4	
ADAM & EVE	**The first man and woman created by God.** Adam and Eve were created righteous, but they sinned by eating the fruit of the forbidden tree. All humankind fell into sin and misery.
CAIN	**The first son of Adam and Eve.** Cain brought God an offering not commanded by God, and he was angry when God rejected his offering. He killed his brother Abel out of jealousy, and he was banished by God.
ABEL	**The second son of Adam and Eve.** Abel brought God a proper offering, and God accepted his offering. Abel was killed by his brother Cain.
SETH	**The third son of Adam and Eve.** Enoch and Noah descended from the line of Seth.
Major Characters from Genesis 5-11	
ENOCH	**A prophet who walked with God.** He did not experience death but was taken away by God.
NOAH	**A righteous man commanded by God to build an ark to escape the Great Flood.** Noah, his wife, and his sons survived along with the animals on the ark.

Major Themes	
CREATION *Genesis 1-2*	God created the world and everything in it. He created humans in His own image. All that God created was good. God rested on the seventh day.
THE FALL *Genesis 3*	God provided Adam and Eve with everything they needed to be happy and holy, but they sinned by eating the forbidden fruit. Because of their sin, all their natural descendants are born in sin. God promised that the offspring of the woman would crush the head of the serpent (Satan).
SONS OF ADAM *Genesis 4 – 5*	The descendants of Adam and Eve began to demonstrate their sinfulness immediately as Cain killed his brother Abel. The descendants of Cain became more violent, but the line of Seth included righteous men such as Enoch and Noah.

THE FLOOD *Genesis 6 – 10*	Because of violence and corruption in the world, God destroyed the earth with a flood, but He spared Noah and his family because of their righteousness.
TOWER OF BABEL *Genesis 11*	People began to build a great city and tower to make a name for themselves. God confused their language, and work on the tower ceased.

How the World Began

CREATION   **GENESIS 1 – 2**

Then God saw everything that He had made, and indeed it was very good.
–Genesis 1:31

The Bible tells us that God created everything, and that He made it all very good. The Bible also tells us that Adam and Eve were created in the image of God — the last and the most special of all creatures made by God.

What does it mean that Adam and Eve were created in the image of God? Does God have physical eyes, ears, hands, and feet like a human? No, God is a Spirit. He does not have a physical body. Adam and Eve were like God in other ways. They were wiser and more knowledgeable than other creatures. They ruled over other creatures and cared for them. These attributes reflected the image of God. God is wise and all-knowing. He is perfectly holy. He rules over all things and cares for all things.

God made a **covenant** with Adam. God required that Adam obey His holy commandments perfectly, and in exchange, God promised to give life to Adam and to all his descendants. We call this promise the **covenant of works**.

THE FALL   **GENESIS 3**

Therefore, just as through one man sin entered the world, and death through sin,
and thus death spread to all men, because all sinned… –Romans 5:12

As we noted in the last section, the Bible tells us that God created everything, and that He made it all very good.

However we know that all things in the earth are not good anymore. There is violence, corruption, illness, and disaster. What went wrong? Adam broke the covenant. He did not completely obey God. Adam and Eve ate the fruit of the tree that God had told them not to eat. They were not hungry; God had provided plenty of other food for them. They simply chose to disobey God.

31

Since Adam was the head of the covenant, his disobedience plunged all mankind into sin and misery. All natural descendants of Adam and Eve were born with a sinful nature, and they were born into a world that was no longer perfectly good.

SONS OF ADAM   GENESIS 4 – 5

Then the LORD said to Cain, "Where is Abel your brother?"
He said, "I do not know. Am I my brother's keeper?" –Genesis 4:9

The effects of the Fall among the descendants of Adam and Eve began almost immediately. Their son Cain murdered his brother Abel. Cain's descendants began a rapid downward spiral. By the fifth generation from Cain, violence had become a way of life. Cain's descendant Lamech's boast is recorded in Genesis 4: "…I have killed a man for wounding me, even a young man for hurting me."

Even as humanity plunged into horrifying sin, God provided hope. The last child mentioned as born to Adam and Eve was named Seth. From the descendants of Seth would one day arise a Savior to redeem all God's chosen people.

THE FLOOD   GENESIS 6 – 10

By faith Noah, being divinely warned of things not yet seen, moved with godly fear,
prepared an ark for the saving of his household, by which he condemned the world and
became heir of the righteousness which is according to faith. –Hebrews 11:7

Within a few generations, mankind had descended into utter ruin. "The earth also was corrupt before God, and the earth was filled with violence" (Genesis 6:11). But one man stood out in contrast to all the corruption around him. Noah was a righteous man, and he found favor with God.

God decided to wipe out the whole world with a flood. But He instructed Noah to build an ark to save himself and his family. Because of Noah's obedience, he was spared from the judgment of God.

As the rains poured down and the waters rose, Noah and his family were sheltered in the haven God had provided for them. When the flood was over, God put a rainbow in the sky as a sign of His promise that He would never again destroy the whole earth with a flood.

Through the story of Noah, we witness God's tenderness toward those who have faith in Him. When God's judgment falls on evil, He provides shelter for His chosen people. Those who love and honor God put their trust in Him knowing that He has mercy on those who fear Him.

For this cause everyone who is godly shall pray to You in a time when You may be found;
Surely in a flood of great waters they shall not come near him.
You are my hiding place; You shall preserve me from trouble;
You shall surround me with songs of deliverance. – Psalm 32:6-7

THE TOWER OF BABEL   GENESIS 11

And they said, "Come, let us build ourselves a city,
and a tower whose top is in the heavens;
let us make a name for ourselves, lest we be scattered abroad
over the face of the whole earth." –Genesis 11:4

The lessons of the Great Flood did not resonate long in the memories of Noah's descendants. They soon began to demonstrate willful rebellion against God. God had instructed them to fill the earth, but in their arrogance, they rejected His commandment. The descendants of Noah were determined to make a name for themselves. They wanted to stay together and dwell in a city filled with their own glory. They began work on a tower that they boasted would reach up to heaven.

God was displeased with their scheme. He knew that human knowledge is heavily dependent on communication, and so He did something simple but highly effective: He made them speak different languages. They could no longer understand each other. They could not share their ideas and solve construction problems amongst themselves.

The grand plan of the arrogant inhabitants of Shinar collapsed abruptly. They gave up building the city and moved away from each other. Soon they filled the whole earth just as God had intended.

Catechism on Creation

Genesis 1 & 2

Q1. Who created the heavens and the earth?

    A. God created the heavens and the earth.

Q2. In how many days did God create the heavens and the earth?

    A. In six days.

Q3. What did God created on the first day?

    A. God created light and divided light from darkness.

Q4. What did God create on the second day?

    A. God created the sky, dividing the waters above from the waters below.

Q5. What did God create on the third day?

    A. God separated sea from dry land. He created plants.

Q6. What did God create on the fourth day?

    A. God created the sun, moon, and stars.

Q7. What did God create on the fifth day?

    A. God created birds and fish.

Q8. What did God create on the sixth day?

    A. God created land animals. He also created Adam and Eve.

Q9. What did God do on the seventh day?

    A. He rested.

Q10. How did God create Adam and Eve different from the animals?

    A. God created Adam and Eve in His own image.

Q11. What covenant did God make with Adam?

A. The covenant of works: Adam must obey God perfectly, and God would provide life for him and his descendants.

Catechism on the Fall

Genesis 3

Q1. Did Adam and Eve keep the covenant of works?

A. No, they sinned against God.

Q2. How did Adam and Eve break the covenant of works?

A. They ate the fruit of the tree from which God had forbidden them to eat.

Q3. What do we call this breaking of the covenant?

A. We call it the Fall, because all humankind fell into sin and misery.

Catechism on the Sons of Adam

Genesis 4 & 5

Q1. Who were the first two sons of Adam and Eve?

A. Cain and Abel.

Q2. Why did God accept Abel's sacrifice?

A. Abel offered the proper sacrifice required by God.

Q3. Why did God reject Cain's sacrifice?

A. Cain offered God an improper sacrifice that God had not commanded.

Q4. What did Cain do to his brother Abel?

A. Cain killed Abel.

Q5. Who was the third son of Adam and Eve?

A. Seth.

Q6. Cain had a descendant named Lamech. What did Lamech boast about?

A. Lamech boasted about violence.

Q7. Who were Lamech's sons?

A. Jabal, Jubal, and Tubal-Cain.

Q8. Seth had a descendant named Enoch. Who was Enoch?

A. Enoch was a prophet who walked with God.

Q9. Who was Enoch's great-grandson?

A. Noah.

Q10. Who were Noah's sons?

A. Shem, Ham, and Japheth.

Catechism on the Flood

Genesis 6 – 10

Q1. How was Noah different from those of his generation?

A. Noah was a righteous man.

Q2. **What did God command Noah to do?**

  A. God commanded Noah to build an ark to save his family from the coming flood.

Q3. **How many of each kind of animal did God tell Noah to take on the ark?**

  A. A male and female pair of every kind, and seven pairs of the animals used for sacrifices.

Q4. **How long did rain fall during the flood?**

  A. Forty days and forty nights.

Q5. **Where did the ark settle after the flood waters receded?**

  A. On Mount Ararat.

Q6. **The rainbow is the sign of God's promise. What did God promise?**

  A. God promised that He would never again destroy the whole earth with a flood.

Catechism on the Tower of Babel

Genesis 11

Q1. **How many languages existed before the Tower of Babel?**

  A. Only one language.

Q2. **Why did the people in the plain of Shinar decide to build a tower?**

  A. To make a name for themselves.

Q3. How did God stop them building the tower?

    A. He caused them to speak different languages so that they could not understand each other.

Q4. What was the tower called?

    A. The Tower of Babel.

Days of Creation Chart

In the beginning, God created the heavens and the earth. – Genesis 1:1

DAY 1	God created light and divided light from darkness.
DAY 2	God created the sky, dividing the waters above from the waters below.
DAY 3	God separated sea from dry land. He created plants.
DAY 4	God created the sun, moon, and stars.
DAY 5	God created birds and fish.
DAY 6	God created land animals. He also created Adam and Eve.
DAY 7	God rested.

Creation Rhyme

On the first day, God made the light,
Divided darkness from the light,
He called one day, the other night –
God saw that it was good. *(clap, clap)*

On the second day, God made the sky,
Where flocks of birds would soon fly by.
Some water low and some up high.
God saw that it was good. *(clap, clap)*

On the third day, God made the land,
Seas drew back to form dry sand,
Trees grew tall at God's command.
God saw that it was good. *(clap, clap)*

On the fourth day, God made the sun,
To shine by day on everyone,
Moon and stars one by one,
God saw that it was good. *(clap, clap)*

On the fifth day, God made the fish,
With gills and fins and tails that swish;
And all the birds that you could wish.
God saw that it was good. *(clap, clap)*

On the sixth day, God made the dogs,
Big giraffes and small hedgehogs,
Slithering worms and slimy frogs.
God saw that it was good. *(clap, clap)*

Then God created something new,
He thought of me;
He thought of you,
He made Adam, then He made Eve too.
God saw that it was good. *(clap, clap)*
God saw that it was good. *(clap, clap)*
It was very, very good.

Family Tree

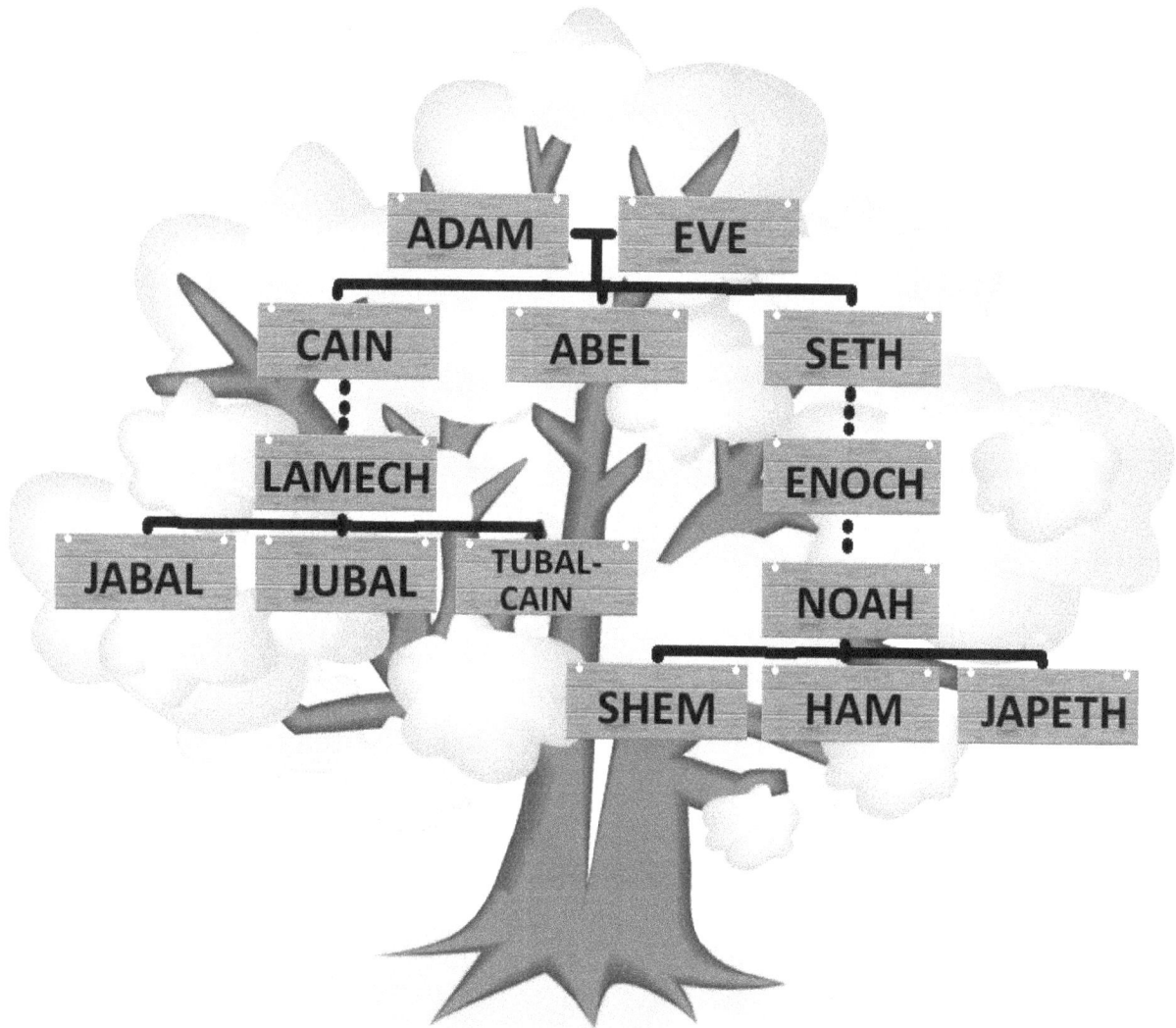

ADAM — EVE

CAIN   ABEL   SETH

LAMECH   ENOCH

JABAL   JUBAL   TUBAL-CAIN   NOAH

SHEM   HAM   JAPETH

Part 3

The Patriarchs

Genesis 12 – 50

You should know...

- the covenant God made with Abraham
- the patriarchs and matriarchs of Genesis:
    - Abraham & Sarah
    - Isaac & Rebekah
    - Jacob, Leah, & Rachel
    - The twelve sons of Jacob

By faith Abraham obeyed when he was called to go out to the place which he would receive as an inheritance. He went out, not knowing where he was going. By faith he dwelt in the land of promise as in a foreign country, dwelling in tents with Isaac and Jacob, the heirs with him of the same promise; for he waited for the city which has foundations, whose builder and maker is God.

- Hebrews 11:8-10

Characters and Themes

Major Characters from Genesis 12-20	
Abram (Abraham)	**Chosen by God to be the father of a nation in covenant with God.** Abram left his home in Ur and traveled to the place God promised to his descendants. God made a covenant with Abram, changing his name to Abraham, and promising him descendants as numerous as the stars in the sky.
Sarai (Sarah)	Abraham's wife and mother of Isaac, the promised son.
Hagar	Sarah's handmaid whom Abraham took as his second wife. Unable to bear children and not believing God's promise, Sarah gave Hagar to her husband so that he could have a son.
Ishmael	**The son of Abraham and Hagar.** Born of unbelief, Ishmael was not the promised son. But since he was a son of Abraham, God still made his descendants into a strong nation.
Lot	Abraham's nephew. After his father Haran (Abraham's brother) died, Lot joined Abraham in the journey to the land God had promised. He settled near Sodom until its destruction. Lot's descendants were the Moabites.
Melchizedek	**King of Salem and priest of the Lord.** Melchizedek blessed Abraham.
Major Characters from Genesis 21-26	
Isaac	**Son of Abraham and Sarah.** He was the long-awaited promised son through whom God would build His chosen nation.
Rebekah	**Isaac's wife.** Rebekah was the sister of Laban and mother of Isaac's twin sons Esau and Jacob.
Major Characters from Genesis 27-36	
Esau	**The firstborn of Isaac and Rebekah's twin sons.** Esau sold his birthright to Jacob and so gave up his rightful claim as Isaac's heir. Esau's descendants were the Edomites.
Jacob (Israel)	**The second of Isaac and Rebekah's twin sons.** He obtained the birthright and blessing through deceit. He married Laban's daughters Leah and Rachel and later also their handmaids Bilhah and Zilpah. He became the father of twelve sons.
Laban	A relative from the family of Abraham and Sarah. **Father of Leah and Rachel.**
Leah	**Older daughter of Laban.** Leah was unloved by Jacob, who was tricked into marrying her instead of her younger sister Rachel.

Rachel	**Younger daughter of Laban.** Jacob worked for Laban for seven years on the promise of marrying her.
Major Characters from Genesis 37-50	
Bilhah & Zilpah	**Handmaids of Leah and Rachel.** Jacob was given these as his wives also, as Leah and Rachel competed with each other for children.
Reuben	**Oldest son of Jacob.** Mother: Leah.
Simeon	**Second son of Jacob.** Mother: Leah
Levi	**Third son of Jacob.** Mother: Leah
Judah	**Fourth son of Jacob.** Mother: Leah
Dan	**Fifth son of Jacob.** Mother: Rachel's handmaid Bilhah
Naphtali	**Sixth son of Jacob.** Mother: Rachel's handmaid Bilhah
Gad	**Seventh son of Jacob.** Mother: Leah's handmaid Zilpah
Asher	**Eighth son of Jacob.** Mother: Leah's handmaid Zilpah
Issachar	**Ninth son of Jacob.** Mother: Leah
Zebulun	**Tenth son of Jacob.** Mother: Leah
Joseph	**Eleventh son of Jacob.** Mother: Rachel
Benjamin	**Twelfth son of Jacob.** Mother: Rachel
Dinah	**Daughter of Jacob and Leah.**
Potiphar	**Officer of Pharaoh in Egypt who bought Joseph as a slave.**
Pharaoh (during Joseph)	**King of Egypt who appointed Joseph as second in command.** He welcomed Joseph's family to Egypt during the famine.

Major Themes	
ABRAHAM *Genesis 12-20*	God made a covenant with Abraham through which someday the Savior would come. In Abraham's descendants, God established His chosen people.
ISAAC *Genesis 21-26*	The long-awaited son Isaac was the beginning of God's fulfillment of His covenant with Abraham.
JACOB *Genesis 27 – 36*	At last the nation of Israel began rapid expansion. The twelve tribes were established by the sons of Jacob. Yet conflict and trouble were common even among God's chosen people, and Jacob wrestled with God.
JOSEPH *Genesis 37-50*	God's providence and sovereignty are displayed in the life of Joseph. Though Joseph suffered severe injustice, God worked through all his trials to protect and provide for Joseph, his family, and many others.

The Patriarchs

ABRAHAM   **GENESIS 12 – 20**

> After these things the word of the LORD came to Abram in a vision, saying,
> "Do not be afraid, Abram. I am your shield, your exceedingly great reward."
> –Genesis 15:1

In Genesis 11, the Bible begins to give us a little background for a man named Abram. At first, we see nothing spectacular about the story. Abram's father was called Terah. Terah had three sons, one of whom died younger than the others and left behind several children, including a son named Lot. Terah's son Abram married a woman named Sarai, but she could not have children.

In chapter 12, we see why the Bible has focused our attention on this seemingly unremarkable family. God called Abram to leave his father's home in Ur and set out on a journey. In those days, there were no maps and no modern roads. There were no cars or planes. Abram did not know where he was going, and the journey was dangerous. However, Abram had faith in God. He obeyed God and set out with his wife, his nephew Lot, and the rest of his household and possessions. There must have been quite a caravan of camels and donkeys hauling wagons filled with tents, food, cooking utensils, clothes, and everything else they would need. There were sheep and goats, and herdsmen to tend them—and the families of the herdsmen too. It was like moving a small town!

God chose Abram for a particular purpose. He was already preparing the world for the arrival of Jesus, the Messiah who would save His people from their sins. He chose Abram to be the father of a nation that would receive God's law and prophets. Eventually Christ Himself would come from the descendants of Abram.

God made a covenant with Abram, declaring:

> No longer shall your name be called Abram, but your name shall be
> Abraham; for I have made you a father of many nations... and I will
> establish My covenant between Me and you and your descendants
> after you in their generations, for an everlasting covenant, to be God
> to you and your descendants after you. – Genesis 17:5,7

49

Now Abraham was one hundred years old when his son Isaac was born to him.
–Genesis 21:5

Although God had promised Abraham a child, Sarai (renamed Sarah by God) was unable to have any children. As Abraham grew old, it seemed less likely that God's promise would be fulfilled. Desperate for an heir, Abraham took a second wife, Sarah's maid Hagar. Although this was a common practice in those days, it was not the right thing to do. Hagar gave Abraham a son named Ishmael, but trouble soon developed between Hagar and Sarah. Hagar was arrogant toward Sarah, and Sarah was angry and jealous. Ishmael was not the child that God had promised.

In time God fulfilled his promise to Abraham. Even in her old age, Sarah gave birth to a son named Isaac. Trouble with Hagar and Ishmael quickly boiled over. Ishmael was cruel to Isaac, and Sarah demanded that Abraham send them away. Abraham was sad, but he did as Sarah asked. Even though Ishmael had been born because of Abraham's unbelief, God still protected and provided for Hagar and Ishmael.

Isaac grew up and married a woman named Rebekah. They had twin sons, Esau and Jacob.

JACOB   **GENESIS 27 – 36**

And He said, "Your name shall no longer be called Jacob, but Israel;
For you have struggled with God and men, and have prevailed."   –Genesis 32:28

Although Esau and Jacob were twins, Esau was still the older son (born a few minutes before his brother), and so by tradition, he had the right to lead the family when their father died. However, Jacob schemed to take his brother's place. Esau cared very little about his **birthright** (his privilege as eldest son). Genesis 25 records that he agreed to sell it to Jacob for a bowl of stew, and he even swore to Jacob that he could have it. However, it appears that Esau did not truly intend to honor his promise. When Isaac made plans to give Esau the blessing intended for the firstborn, Esau never mentioned that he had sold his birthright to his brother.

With the help of his mother Rebekah, Jacob tricked his father Isaac into giving the blessing to him instead of to Esau. When Esau found that he had indeed been deprived of his birthright, he fell into a rage. Jacob was frightened and ran away.

Alone in the desert, Jacob fell asleep and dreamed of a ladder that reached to heaven with angels ascending and descending on it. God spoke to Jacob in the dream, assuring him, "Behold I am with you and will keep you wherever you go" (Genesis 28:15).

Encouraged by the vision, Jacob continued on and found his uncle Laban in the city of Haran. However, Jacob soon fell victim to a plot very much like the one he had used to obtain his birthright. Laban tricked Jacob into marrying his daughter Leah instead of Rachel, the one that Jacob wanted to marry. Then Laban offered to let Jacob marry Rachel as well. Just as there had been great trouble because of Abraham marrying two wives, the household of Jacob soon fell into turmoil because of jealousy between Leah and Rachel. Leah had children, but Rachel did not. Both wives convinced Jacob to also marry their handmaids, Bilhah and Zilpah, as they competed with each other to have children. In the end, Jacob had twelve sons: Reuben, Simeon, Levi, Judah, Dan, Naphtali, Gad, Asher, Issachar, Zebulun, Joseph, and Benjamin. He also had a daughter named Dinah.

Jacob eventually returned to his home and made peace with his brother Esau. God promised His blessing on the household of Jacob, and He gave Jacob the name **Israel**.

JOSEPH   GENESIS 37 – 50

> But Joseph said to them, "Do not be afraid, for am I in the place of God?
> But as for you, you meant evil against me; but God meant it for good, in order
> to bring it about as it is this day, to save many people alive." –Genesis 50:19-20

The story of Joseph tells us about God's sovereign goodness even in difficult circumstances. Jacob loved Joseph more than he loved his other children. Joseph's brothers were jealous of the attention Joseph received from their father. They secretly sold Joseph into slavery in Egypt.

Joseph endured many difficulties in Egypt. He was even imprisoned on false charges! However, Joseph trusted God, and God delivered him from prison. Eventually Joseph became a high official in Egypt, second only to Pharaoh himself.

When a famine struck the land, Joseph's brothers came to Egypt to buy food. They were shocked to discover that their brother Joseph had become a powerful man in Egypt. They were afraid that he would take revenge on them for selling him into slavery.

Joseph forgave his brothers. He declared that God had used even their wicked intentions for good. He brought his father and brothers to live with him in Egypt so that they would not die in the famine.

CONCLUSION

**O LORD God of Abraham, Isaac, and Israel, our fathers,
keep this forever in the intent of the thoughts of the heart of Your people,
and fix their heart toward You. —I Chronicles 29:18**

Stories in the Bible that tell us about the lives of the patriarchs – Abraham, Isaac, Jacob, and his twelve sons – tell us many important things. We learn that God chose Abraham and his descendants out of all the families on earth. God made a covenant with them. He taught them to honor Him and obey Him. He promised that one day the whole earth would be blessed through them (Genesis 18:18).

Through these Bible stories, we also realize that the patriarchs were not perfect. Sometimes they made mistakes; sometimes they sinned. But God was patient with them, forgiving their sins and helping them trust in Him more fully.

God is sovereign over all. He is able to use even our bad decisions for His own good purposes. Jacob's household was troubled with jealousy between his wives, yet the descendants of Jacob became the founders of the twelve tribes of Israel. Joseph's brothers sold him as a slave, but God raised him up in Egypt to become powerful and enabled him to save the lives of many people from famine, including his own family.

Life is often messy and difficult, and people sin against God. But even when we cannot understand, God is working all things together for good (Romans 8:28). He is always faithful to His covenant.

Catechism on Abraham

Q1. Who was Abram's father?

A. Abram's father was Terah.

Q2. Who was Lot?

A. Lot was Abram's nephew.

Q3. Who was Sarai?

A. Sarai was Abram's wife.

Q4. What did God call Abram to do?

A. God called Abram to leave his father's house and go to a land He would show him.

Q5. Where did Lot settle in Canaan?

A. Lot settled in the wicked city of Sodom.

Q6. What did God do to Sodom and Gomorrah because of their wickedness?

A. He destroyed them.

Q7. Was Lot destroyed in Sodom?

A. No, God rescued Lot before destroying the wicked cities.

Q8. God promised Abram and Sarai a child. Did they wait faithfully for God?

A. No, Abram took Hagar as his wife to have a child.

Q9. What was the name of Abram's son with Hagar?

A. His name was Ishmael.

Q10. Was Ishmael God's promised son?

  A. No.

Q11. God fulfilled His promise to give Abram and Sarai a son. What was their son's name?

  A. His name was Isaac.

Q12. God changed Abram and Sarai's names. What did He call them?

  A. God called them Abraham and Sarah.

Q13. God chose Abraham and his descendants as His people, and He made a covenant with them. What was the sign of the covenant?

  A. The sign of the covenant was circumcision.

Catechism on Isaac

Genesis 21 – 26

Q1. How old were Abraham and Sarah when Isaac was born?

  A. Abraham was 100 years old, and Sarah was 90 years old.

Q2. What was the name of Isaac's wife?

  A. Her name was Rebekah.

Q3. Isaac and Rebekah had twin sons. What were their sons' names?

  A. Esau and Jacob.

Catechism on Jacob

Genesis 27 – 36

Q1. Jacob was the younger of the twin sons of Isaac and Rebekah. How did he receive the birthright?

    A. He bought the birthright from Esau for a bowl of stew. Then he tricked his father into giving him the blessing.

Q2. Why did Jacob run away from home?

    A. He was afraid Esau would kill him.

Q3. Where did Jacob go when he ran away from home?

    A. He went to live with his uncle Laban.

Q4. Why did Jacob marry both Leah and Rachel?

    A. Laban tricked Jacob into marrying Leah when he wanted to marry Rachel and then gave him Rachel too.

Q5. How many sons did Jacob have?

    A. Jacob had twelve sons.

Q6. What were the names of Jacob's sons?

    A. Their names were Reuben, Simeon, Levi, Judah, Dan, Naphtali, Gad, Asher, Issachar, Zebulun, Joseph, and Benjamin.

Q7. God gave Jacob a new name. What was his new name?

    A. God named him Israel.

Catechism on Joseph

Q1. Why were Joseph's brothers jealous of him?

A. Their father Jacob loved Joseph more than he loved his other sons.

Q2. What did Joseph's brothers do to him?

A. They sold him into slavery in Egypt.

Q3. Did Joseph have an easy life in Egypt?

A. No, he was a slave and then was imprisoned on false charges.

Q4. When Joseph told the Pharaoh the meaning of his dream, what happened?

A. Pharaoh released him from prison and made him a powerful official in Egypt.

Q5. How did Joseph meet his brothers again?

A. They came to Egypt to buy food during a famine.

Q6. Did Joseph take revenge on his brothers?

A. No, he forgave them. He brought them to live with him in Egypt, and he provided food for them during the famine.

Twelve Sons of Jacob Chart

For He established a testimony in Jacob,
And appointed a law in Israel,
Which He commanded our fathers,
That they should make them known to their children.
– Psalm 78:5

SONS OF JACOB
Reuben
Simeon
Levi
Judah
Dan
Naphtali
Gad
Asher
Issachar
Zebulun
Joseph
Benjamin

Patriarchs & Matriarchs Rhyme

Patriarchs and matriarchs,
Can you recall?
Patriarchs and matriarchs,
Let's say them all!

Abram and **Sarai**—
God changed their names.
Abraham and **Sarah**—
That's who they became.

Hagar's son was **Ishmael**,
Was he the chosen one?
No! **Isaac** was born to **Sarah**,
Isaac was the chosen son!

Isaac married **Rebekah**,
Jacob and **Esau** born one day.
Jacob stole the birthright,
And he ran far away.

Jacob wanted **Rachel**
But he married **Leah** too.
God changed his name to
Israel,
His family quickly grew.

His sons were...
    Reuben, **Simeon**,
    Levi, **Judah**,
    Dan, **Naphtali**,
    Gad, **Asher**,
    Issachar, **Zebulun**,
    Joseph, and **Benjamin**.

Could you remember those if someone asked?
Could you say them really fast?

    Abraham and Sarah!
    Isaac and Rebekah!
    Jacob, Rachel, Leah!
      Reuben, Simeon,
      Levi, Judah,
      Dan, Naphtali,
      Gad, Asher,
      Issachar, Zebulun,
      Joseph, and Benjamin.

Patriarchs and matriarchs —
We can recall!
Patriarchs and matriarchs —
We said them all!

Family Tree

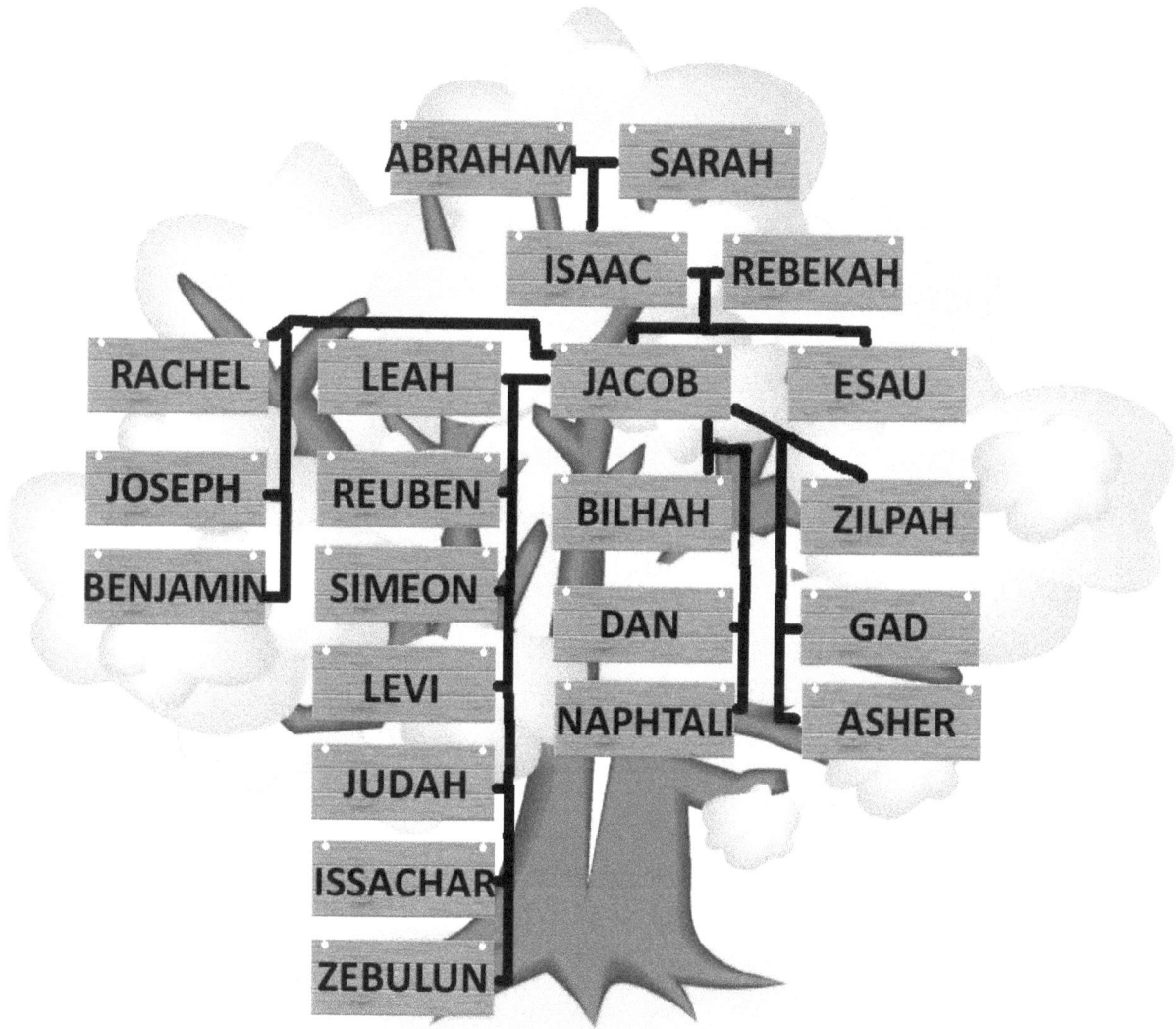

61

Part 4

The Exodus

Exodus – Deuteronomy

You should know...

- the Ten Plagues of Egypt
- the Twelve Tribes of Israel

Then Moses and the children of Israel sang this song to the LORD, and spoke saying:

"I will sing to the LORD,
For He has triumphed gloriously!
The horse and rider
He has thrown into the sea!
The LORD is my strength and song,
And He has become my salvation;
He is my God, and I will praise Him;
My father's God, and I will exalt Him."

- Exodus 15:1-2

Characters and Themes

	Major Characters from Exodus 1-15	
Moses	**Chosen by God to lead the His people out of Egypt to the Promised Land.** Moses received God's law and gave it to the Israelites so that they would know how to honor and obey God.	
Miriam	**Moses' older sister.** Miriam helped save Moses' life when he was a baby, and later she was a prophetess and a leader among the women of Israel.	
Aaron	**Moses' brother.** Aaron accompanied Moses in confronting Pharaoh. God later appointed Aaron and his sons as priests over Israel.	
Pharaoh (during Moses)	**The king of Egypt who kept the Israelites in slavery.** Pharaoh enjoyed the free labor provided by slaves, and he repeatedly refused to let God's people go.	
	Major Characters from Exodus 16 – Deuteronomy 34	
Joshua	**A leader among the Israelites.** Joshua was one of the twelve spies sent into Canaan and one of only two who demonstrated faith in the promises of God. God chose Joshua to succeed Moses as leader of His people.	
Jethro	**Moses' father-in-law.** Briefly introduced in the first part of Exodus as the father of Moses' wife Zipporah, Jethro took on an advisory role to Moses, suggesting ways to set up an effective government for the Israelites.	
Korah	**A rebel in the Israelite camp** who attempted to overthrow Moses.	
Balaam	**A prophet of God.** King Balak attempted to bribe Balaam to curse the Israelites. God refused to permit Balaam to curse His people, and yet Balaam was unfaithful to God, giving advice to Balak about how to bring the anger of God on the Israelites.	
Caleb	**A faithful leader in the Israelite community.** Caleb was one of the faithful spies who gave a good report about the Promised Land and encouraged the Israelites to trust in God's promises.	

Major Themes	
THE TEN PLAGUES *Exodus 1 – 12*	When Pharaoh would not release God's people from slavery in Egypt, God responded with miraculous signs. God demonstrated His sovereign power and His faithfulness to the covenant made with Abraham.
THE RED SEA *Exodus 13 – 15*	When Pharaoh again pursued the Israelites, God saved His people by parting the Red Sea. This "baptism" of His people marked the end of their old life of slavery and put them on the path to the Promised Land as a people set apart by God.
THE DESERT *Exodus 16 -* *Deuteronomy 34*	The journey toward the Promised Land was fraught with difficulty. God tested His people, and over and over they failed to demonstrate faith in Him. God disciplined them, but He did not give up on them. He gave them the Law that would guide them for generations, and He dwelled among them in the Tabernacle.

The Exodus

THE TEN PLAGUES   **EXODUS 1 – 12**

And the Lord said, "I have surely seen the oppression of My people who are in Egypt, And have heard their cry because of their taskmasters, for I know their sorrows."
– Exodus 3:7

The book of Genesis closed with Joseph and his brothers living in Egypt to escape famine. The book of Exodus continued the story as Joseph and his brothers passed away, but their descendants multiplied in Egypt. God blessed the Israelites (also called the *Hebrews*), and soon the Egyptian Pharaoh (a different Pharaoh from the one who had welcomed the Israelites into Egypt) began to see their ever-expanding population as a threat. Pharaoh ordered the Israelite population enslaved and tormented. He even ordered that male children born to Israelite families be killed so that the population of Israelites would decrease.

God saw the distress of His people in Egypt, and He chose Moses to lead them to freedom. Born to an Israelite family but raised in Pharaoh's palace, Moses was uniquely gifted to lead the Israelites and to challenge Pharaoh. God called to Moses out of a burning bush and told him to go with his brother Aaron to stand before Pharaoh and demand that Pharaoh let God's people go to worship Him in the wilderness. Pharaoh suspected that the Israelites, once freed, would never return. He wanted to keep his slaves at work. He refused to allow the Israelites to leave.

Pharaoh believed that his power and the power of the Egyptian gods would prevail. However, God sent plagues on Egypt that proved that only the Lord rules over heaven and earth. The first plagues (the Nile turning to blood, frogs, gnats, and flies descending on Egypt) demonstrated God's power but did little damage to Egypt. After each plague God sent Moses to demand that Pharaoh let God's people go, but Pharaoh always refused. As Pharaoh grew more stubborn, the plagues became more severe. Livestock died. People became sick. Hail and locust destroyed crops. In a last ominous warning, darkness fell over all Egypt except in the part of the land in which the Israelites lived.

After nine plagues, Pharaoh still refused to let God's people go. God sent the tenth and final plague that killed the firstborn of all Egypt. Only the Israelites were spared, for they had put the blood of a lamb on their doorposts, and the judgment of God passed over them. Pharaoh finally relented and let God's people go free.

God proved that He is more powerful than any earthly king. The pagan gods could not help the Egyptians, because only the Lord is God.

Hear, O Israel, the LORD our God, the LORD is one! – Deuteronomy 6:4

THE RED SEA   EXODUS 13 – 15

**For the horses of Pharaoh went with his chariots and his horsemen into the sea,
and the LORD brought back the waters of the sea upon them.
But the children of Israel went on dry land in the midst of the sea.
–Exodus 15:19**

God delivered His people from slavery in Egypt, and He protected and cared for them as they set out on their long journey to Canaan, the land He had promised to Abraham. God went ahead of them as a pillar of cloud during the day and a pillar fire during the night. Every day and every night, the Israelites could look up and see God leading them.

Back in Egypt, Pharaoh quickly forgot the lessons he had learned from the plagues. He became greedy. He wanted his slaves back to work for him. He sent his army chasing after the Israelites to capture them and drag them back to Egypt. The army caught up with the Israelites at the Red Sea.

When the Israelites saw the army closing in behind them, they panicked and cried out in fear to Moses. Even though they had seen God's mighty power rescue them in Egypt and even though they saw God leading them every day, they still did not trust Him as they should.

In spite of His people's lack of confidence, God quickly rescued them. He caused the waters of the Red Sea to divide so that the Israelites could walk through the sea on dry ground. When the Egyptians tried to follow them, the waters of the Red Sea closed over them and swept them away.

God never abandons His people. When He calls us, He also leads us, provides for us, and protects us.

Now, O Israel, listen to the statutes and judgments which I teach you to observe, that you may live, and go in and possess the land which the LORD God of your fathers is giving you. – Deuteronomy 4:1

As the Israelites traveled through the desert toward Canaan, God continued to lead them and care for them. He miraculously provided food and water for all the thousands of people in the Israelite camp. He protected them from attacks by hostile nations.

The most important way in which God provided for His people, however, was not in food, water, or clothing. God's greatest gift to His people was His own presence and His Word. He instructed Moses in building the Tabernacle, a large tent structure in which the people of God could gather to worship Him. At Mount Sinai, He gave them His laws written on stone tablets. The stone tablets, a jar of manna (the miracle food provided by God), and Aaron's staff were all placed within the **Ark of the Covenant**, a gold-covered box used in the worship of God in the Tabernacle. These things served to remind the Israelites for generations that they belonged to God.

With God dwelling among them in the Tabernacle, and with God's laws written on stone in the Ark of the Covenant, and with God's miraculous manna feeding them, you might imagine that the people of Israel loved and honored God every day. However, the Israelites were sinners just like you and me. They complained and rebelled against God. Even as God was giving Moses the commandments, the Israelites made a golden calf and worshiped it. Later they complained that manna was boring, and they demanded that God provide them with meat. Men such as Korah who were jealous of Moses' authority tried to overthrow him.

Just as the patriarchs in the book of Genesis sinned against God, the people of Israel in the book of Exodus also sinned against God. God was often angry with them, but He was still faithful to His covenant.

Catechism on the Ten Plagues of Egypt

Exodus 1 – 12

Q1. Why was the new Pharaoh in Egypt afraid of the Israelites?

    A. The Israelites population was growing, and Pharaoh feared that they might join his enemies and fight against him.

Q2. What did Pharaoh do to the Israelites?

    A. He made the Israelites work as slaves, and he ordered their male babies to be killed.

Q3. How did Moses grow up?

    A. He was born as a slave in Egypt but raised as a prince by Pharaoh's daughter.

Q4. How did God call Moses?

    A. He called to Moses from a burning bush.

Q5. How did God identify Himself to Moses?

    A. He said, "I am the God of your father – the God of Abraham, the God of Isaac, and the God of Jacob."

Q6. What did God call Moses to do?

    A. God called Moses to confront Pharaoh and command him to let God's people go.

Q7. What name did God call Himself?

    A. God called Himself, "I AM WHO I AM."

Q8. Who was Aaron?

A. Aaron was Moses' brother. He went with Moses to confront Pharaoh.

Q9. Did Pharaoh listen to Moses and Aaron?

A. No, Pharaoh refused to let God's people go.

Q10. How many plagues did God send on Egypt?

A. God sent ten plagues: blood, frogs, gnats, flies, death of livestock, boils, hail, locust, darkness, and the death of the firstborn.

Q11. How did God protect His people from the plague of the death of the firstborn?

A. God instructed them to kill a lamb and put its blood on their doorposts. When God saw the blood on the doorposts, He passed over the house and spared all those inside.

Q12. What happened after the last plague?

A. Pharaoh finally allowed the Israelites to leave Egypt.

Q13. What feast did God command the Israelites to keep to remember the night they left Egypt?

A. He told them to keep the Passover.

Catechism on the Red Sea

Exodus 13 – 15

Q1. How did God lead the Israelites toward the Red Sea?

A. He went before them by day as a pillar of cloud and at night as a pillar of fire.

Q2. Why did Pharaoh chase after the Israelites?

    A. He wanted to bring them back to work as slaves again.

Q3. How did Pharaoh trap the Israelites?

    A. He brought his army behind them while they were on the edge of the Red Sea.

Q4. How did God deliver the Israelites?

    A. God split apart the Red Sea so that the Israelites could walk through on dry ground.

Q5. How did God fight against the Egyptians?

    A. God caused their chariot wheels to fall off so that they could not catch up to the Israelites. Then He caused the waters of the sea to go back and cover them.

Q6. How did the Israelites celebrate?

    A. Moses and his sister Miriam sang a song praising the Lord for delivering His people from Pharaoh's army.

Catechism on the Desert

Exodus 16 – Deuteronomy 34

Q1. How did God feed His people in the desert?

    A. He gave them manna from heaven, and sometimes He sent quail into the camp.

Q2. How did God give His people water?

    A. He sweetened bitter water, and He made water gush from a rock.

Q3. Were the people thankful for God's provision?

    A. No, they complained and said they wanted to go back to Egypt.

Q4. What sin did Korah commit?

    A. Korah led a rebellion to overthrow Moses, but God destroyed him and his followers.

Q5. Who was Balaam?

    A. Balaam was a prophet of God hired by Balak, the king of Moab, to curse the Israelites.

Q6. Did Balaam curse the Israelites as Balak requested?

    A. No, Balaam wanted to do as Balak asked, but God refused to allow Balaam to curse His people. He blessed them instead.

Ten Plagues of Egypt Chart

Go in, tell Pharaoh king of Egypt to let the children of Israel
go out of his land. – Exodus 6:11

PLAGUES OF EGYPT	
	Water turned into blood
	Frogs
	Gnats
	Flies
	Death of livestock

	Boils
	Hail
	Locust
	Darkness
	Death of the firstborn

Twelve Tribes of Israel Chart

Blessed is the nation whose God is the LORD,
The people He has chosen as His own inheritance.
– Psalm 33:12

TRIBES OF ISRAEL
Reuben
Simeon
Levi
Judah
Dan
Naphtali
Gad
Asher
Issachar
Zebulon
Joseph (Ephraim & Manasseh)
Benjamin

Ten Plagues Rhyme

God said to Pharaoh,
"Let my people go!"
Pharaoh's heart was hard,
And he said, "NO!"

Moses struck the Nile;
It turned into blood;
Out of the river
Frogs came like a flood.

Did Pharaoh let God's people go?
His heart was hard, and he said, "NO!"

Moses struck the ground;
Gnats formed from the sand,
Flies swarmed through the palace,
Covered all the land.

Did Pharaoh let God's people go?
His heart was hard, and he said, "NO!"

In Egypt all the livestock died
Because of Pharaoh's sin,
The Egyptians were afflicted
With boils on their skin.

Did Pharaoh let God's people go?
His heart was hard,
And he said, "NO!"

Hail destroyed the crops;
Locust ate the rest;
Darkness fell in daytime;
Egypt was distressed.

Did Pharaoh let God's people go?
His heart was hard, and he said, "NO!"

Nine times did God send plagues to warn,
Nine times did Pharaoh act with scorn,
The tenth plague made all Egypt mourn -
The midnight death of their firstborn.

Was Pharaoh still proud? Did he say no?
He told God's people, "GO! GO! GO!"

Exodus Journey Map

Now this is the commandment, and these are the statutes and judgments which the LORD your God has commanded to teach you, that you may observe them in the land which you are crossing over to possess.
– Deuteronomy 6:1

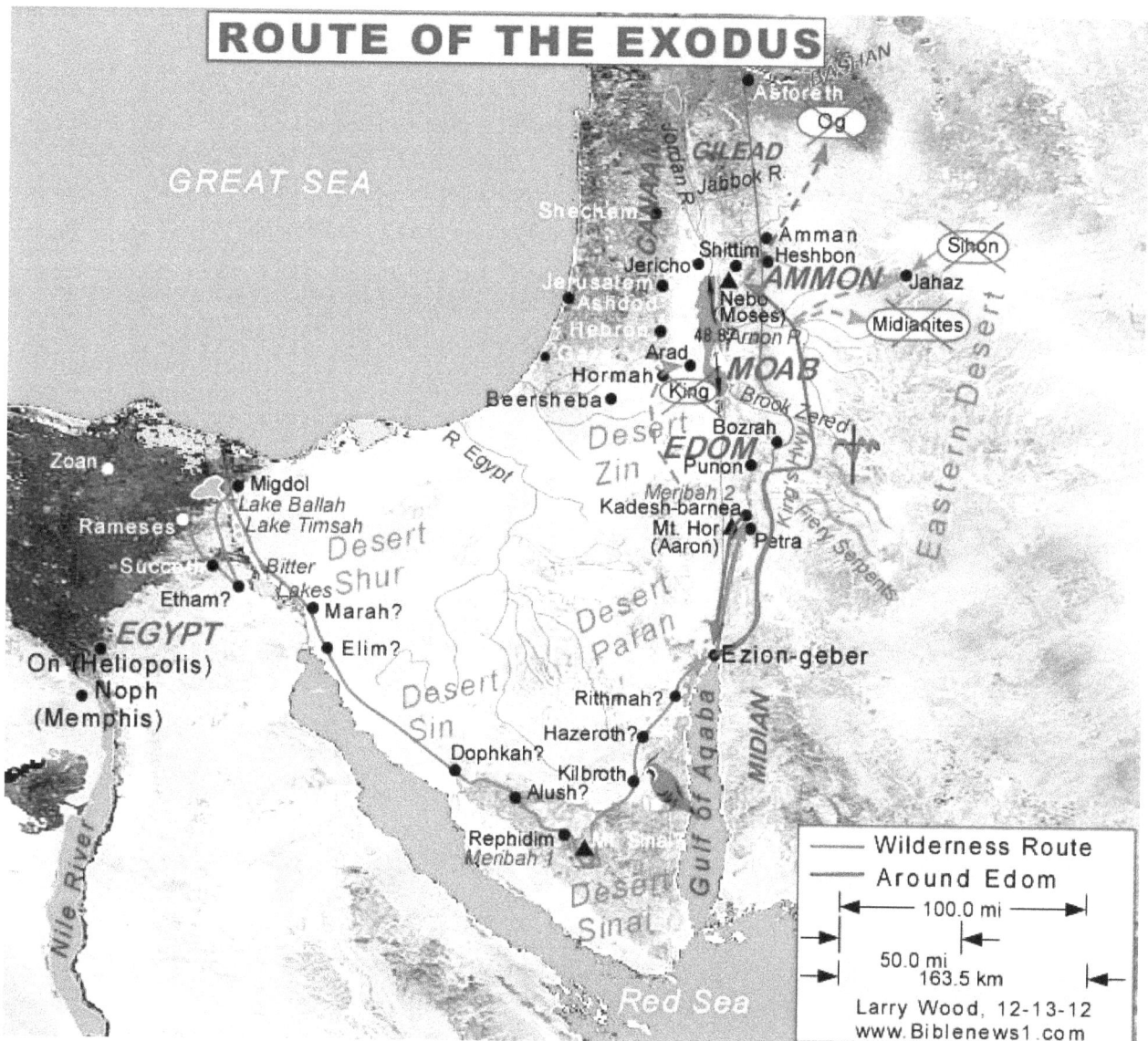

Moses led the Israelites out of Egypt into the Promised Land.

Part 5

The Law

Exodus – Deuteronomy

You should know...

- the Ten Commandments
- the three types of laws
- the purpose of the Tabernacle
- the purpose of the Ark of the Covenant
- the Feasts

How can a young man cleanse his way?
By taking heed according to Your word.
With my whole heart I have sought You;
Oh, let me not wander from Your commandments!
Your word I have hidden in my heart,
That I might not sin against You.
Blessed are You, O LORD!
Teach me Your statutes.

- Psalm 119:9-12

The Law

TYPES OF LAWS

Many people shall come and say,
"Come, and let us go up to the mountain of the LORD,
To the house of the God of Jacob;
He will teach us His ways,
And we shall walk in His paths."
For out of Zion shall go forth the law,
And the word of the Lord from Jerusalem.
–Isaiah 2:3

In Part 4 we discussed the story of Moses. God delivered His people from slavery in Egypt, and He appointed Moses to lead them to the Promised Land. While the Israelites traveled through the desert, God provided food and water for them. But He gave them something even more wonderful than miraculous food and water; He gave them His Law. God revealed His Law to Moses, so that the Israelites would always know what they should do to honor and serve the Lord.

God gave His people many laws about many things. In fact, scholars later counted 613 laws! Some laws instructed God's people not to commit murder. Some laws instructed them about how to conduct special sacrifices. Some laws told them what to do with a vicious animal that attacked someone in the community.

So how do we organize and make sense of all these laws? The Westminster Confession of Faith tells us that there are three main categories:

1. **Moral Law – God's rules of perfect righteousness, summarized in the Ten Commandments.** The Moral Law gives us direction that applies to all people every day in every place. For example, God commands us, "You shall not murder." Whether you lived in the Israelite camp and listened to Moses read this commandment from the stone tablets, or whether you live in Tulsa, Oklahoma, today and you read this commandment on your computer, the rule applies exactly the same.

2. **Ceremonial Law – God's laws for worship, especially sacrifices and feasts.** In the Ceremonial Law God carefully set out rules for Israel's worship. He gave instructions about building the Tabernacle as a meeting place between God and His people. He gave regulations about which sacrifices should be offered and what feasts should be observed. The Ceremonial Law taught the Israelites to look forward in faith to the Messiah who one day would redeem all His people from their sins. We do not keep the Ceremonial Law in the same way today as the Israelites did in the Old Testament era, because the Ceremonial Law was fulfilled in Christ. For example, today we do not sacrifice animals, because Christ is the sacrifice for our sins.

3. **Judicial Law – God's laws giving guidelines on community life including political matters.** The Judicial Law (also called **Civil Law**) provided rules for living together in society. Many of the rules were safety regulations. For example, the Israelites were required to build a wall around each roof so that people would not fall off the roof. This was important because people in that region used the roofs of their houses as balconies on which to eat and rest. It would have been very dangerous for people to be on a roof that did not have a wall! Today we keep the **general equity** of the Judicial Law. In some regions of the world today, we do not build walls around the roof because people do not eat and sleep on the roof. But we should still consider the purpose of God's laws and apply this purpose to our lives today. For example, we build walls around balconies to prevent people from falling off the balcony.

THE TEN COMMANDMENTS

> **Then the LORD said to Moses, "Come up to Me on the mountain and be there; and I will give you tablets of stone, and the law and commandments which I have written, that you may teach them." —Exodus 24:12**

The Ten Commandments contain a summary of the Moral Law. Each commandment tells us an important principle about how to love God and our neighbor. The commandments are arranged in a specific order. We begin with laws about our relationship to God, and then we transition to laws which tell us how we should treat other people.

Let's consider each of the Ten Commandments (Exodus 20):

1. **You shall have no other gods before Me.** This commandment teaches us that we must acknowledge that God is the only true God, and that we must accept His authority over us. Only when we begin by acknowledging God's authority can we move on toward obeying His commands.

2. **You shall not make for yourself a carved image – any likeness of anything that is in heaven above or that is in the earth beneath, or that is in the water under the earth; you shall not bow down to them nor serve them. For I, the LORD your God, am a jealous God, visiting the iniquity of the fathers upon the children to the third and fourth generations of those who hate Me, but showing mercy to thousands, to those who love Me and keep My commandments.** This commandment instructs us to worship God in the manner in which God has commanded us to worship Him.

3. **You shall not take the name of the LORD your God in vain, for the LORD will not hold him guiltless who takes His name in vain.** God forbids us from misusing His name. We should honor God and show respect to Him and to His Word.

4. **Remember the Sabbath day, to keep it holy. Six days you shall labor and do all your work, but the seventh day is the Sabbath of the LORD your God. In it you shall do no work: you, nor your son, nor your daughter, nor your male servant, nor your female servant, nor your cattle, nor your stranger who is within your gates. For in six days the LORD made the heavens and the earth, the sea, and all that is in them, and rested on the seventh day. Therefore, the LORD blessed the Sabbath day and hallowed it.** God commands us to spend the Sabbath (which we now celebrate on Sunday) in worship and rest. We should keep the Sabbath holy, and we should also help other people keep the Sabbath holy.

5. **Honor your father and your mother, that your days may be long upon the land which the LORD your God is giving you.** Just as the first commandment taught us to respect God's authority, this commandment teaches us to respect the authority of those whom God has placed over us (parents, pastors, teachers, and others).

6. **You shall not murder.** Life is a gift from God. We should never take away someone's life unlawfully.

7. **You shall not commit adultery.** God created marriage as a special union between one man (the husband) and one woman (the wife). This union must be kept pure and only between the husband and wife.

8. **You shall not steal.** God instructs us to obtain things in a lawful and proper way. We should not hurt other people by taking away things that rightfully belong to them.

9. **You shall not bear false witness against your neighbor.** This commandment teaches us to be truthful, especially in things we say about other people.

10. **You shall not covet your neighbor's house; you shall not covet your neighbor's wife, nor his male servant, nor his female servant, nor his ox, nor his donkey, nor anything that is your neighbor's.** While other commandments discuss our behavior, this commandment focuses more on the attitude of the heart. We should be content with what we have, and we should not be envious of other people.

THE TABERNACLE

How lovely is Your tabernacle, O LORD of hosts!
—Psalm 84:1

God gave Moses many laws instructing the Israelites about offering sacrifices and holding feasts. With so many ceremonial laws to observe, the Israelites needed a place of worship with an altar and other ceremonial furnishings. God instructed the Israelites to build a **Tabernacle** as their place of worship.

Imagine that you live in the time of Moses, and you have been chosen to serve the Lord as a priest. As you approach the Tabernacle to carry out your priestly duties, the first thing you see is a large wall made of linen cloth supported by pillars. Going through the gateway, you find yourself in a courtyard containing an altar and a basin. The altar is used for offering sacrifices, and the basin is used in ceremonial washing.

Behind the altar and the basin stands a large tent. Entering the tent, you see a golden candlestick on your left and a table for showbread on your right. Straight in front of you is a small incense altar.

A thick, heavy curtain hangs beyond the incense altar, but you must never go behind it! That is the Most Holy Place, and it contains the **Ark of the Covenant**. The Ark of the Covenant contains three very special things: Aaron's rod, a jar of manna, and the tablets containing the Ten Commandments. Only specially chosen priests on very special days may venture into the Most Holy Place!

The arrangement of the Tabernacle reminds us how we approach God. We can only come to God through Jesus' sacrifice and the washing away of our sins. Before Jesus died on the cross, no one except a few specially chose priests could approach God in the Most Holy Place. But now all God's people are invited to be near to God. He has forgiven our sins and made us holy in Christ. We can approach Him with confidence.

Because the Israelites were traveling through the desert, the entire Tabernacle was made of tent materials. When the Israelites moved from one place to another, the priests took the Tabernacle down, carried it to the new location, and set it up again. Even after the Israelites settled in the Promised Land, they continued to use the Tabernacle for many generations.

THE FEASTS

So this day shall be a memorial; and you shall keep it as a feast to the LORD throughout your generations. You shall keep it as a feast by an everlasting ordinance. –Exodus 12:14

God gave the Israelites special holidays. Each holiday had a different purpose. Some were sad days for confessing sin. Some were happy days for rejoicing in God's goodness. Some were days to remember important events. As the community of Israel progressed through the year, each holiday reminded them to honor and serve the Lord. They remembered their sins, God's forgiveness, and many wonderful things God had done for them.

Let's review the seven holidays that God gave the Israelites in the Law:

1. **Feast of Passover** – This feast reminded the Israelites that God brought them out of slavery. They traveled to Jerusalem, ate a special meal to remember their days of slavery, and thanked God for His deliverance. They remembered that blood of a lamb marked the doorposts of the homes where God protected His people from judgment, and now we remember that the blood of Jesus protects us from the judgment of God.

2. **Feast of Unleavened Bread** – In the Bible, yeast symbolized sin. During the Feast of Unleavened Bread, the Israelites removed all yeast from their homes and ate bread made without yeast. This reminded them to keep themselves from sin.

3. **Feast of First Fruits** – This feast was held in the spring. Priests would present to God the first of the crops and a lamb. The Israelites were reminded to trust God's provision.

4. **Feast of Pentecost** – This feast is also called the **Feast of Weeks**. The Israelites thanked God for the wheat harvest and traveled to the Temple in Jerusalem to make offerings to the Lord.

5. **Day of Atonement** – On this holy day, the Israelites were called to mourn for their sins. They fasted, prayed, and offered sacrifices.

6. **Feast of Trumpets** – Announced with the blowing of rams' horns, the Feast of Trumpets heralded the beginning of a new year for the Israelite community. They celebrated with a special assembly, prayers, and sacrifices.

7. **Feast of Tabernacles** – This feast was a camping celebration! The Israelites built shelters outside their homes to sleep in while they celebrated with special assemblies and sacrifices. After the Israelites settled in the Promised Land, this feast reminded them of God's provision as they traveled through the desert camping in tents.

These festivals were given to the Israelites in the Law. Other holidays were added later to commemorate important events. Purim, for example, celebrated the day God delivered the Israelites from the evil plans of Haman (told in the book of Esther), and Hanukkah reminded them of God's help during the dark years between the Old Testament and New Testament when the Israelites were persecuted by Antiochus Epiphanes.

Catechism on the Types of Law

Q1. What are the three main categories of the Law?

 A. The three categories of the law are: Moral Law, Ceremonial Law, and Judicial (or Civil) Law.

Q2. What is contained in the Moral Law?

 A. The Moral Law contains God's rules of perfect righteousness.

Q3. Where is the Moral Law summarized?

 A. The Moral Law is summarized in the Ten Commandments.

Q4. What is contained in the Ceremonial Law?

 A. The Ceremonial Law contains God's rules for worship, especially sacrifices and feasts.

Q5. What is contained in the Judicial (Civil) Law?

 A. The Judicial (Civil) Law contains God's rules for community life.

Catechism on the Ten Commandments

Q1. What is the first commandment?

 A. The first commandment is: *You shall have no other gods before Me.*

Q2. What does the first commandment teach us?

    A. The first commandment teaches us that we must acknowledge that God is the only true God, and that we must accept His authority over us.

Q3. What is the second commandment?

    A. The second commandment is: *You shall not make for yourself a carved image.*

Q4. What does the second commandment teach us?

    A. The second commandment teaches us to worship God in the manner God has commanded us to worship Him.

Q5. What is the third commandment?

    A. The third commandment is: *You shall not take the name of the LORD your God in vain.*

Q6. What does the third commandment teach us?

    A. The third commandment teaches us to honor God and to respect His name.

Q7. What is the fourth commandment?

    A. The fourth commandment is: *Remember the Sabbath day, to keep it holy.*

Q8. What does the fourth commandment teach us?

    A. The fourth commandment teaches us to devote the Sabbath day to God in worship and rest.

Q9. What is the fifth commandment?

    A. The fifth commandment is: *Honor your father and your mother.*

Q10. What does the fifth commandment teach us?

    A. The fifth commandment teaches us to respect the authority of those whom God has placed over us.

Q11. What is the sixth commandment?

A. The sixth commandment is: *You shall not murder.*

Q12. What does the sixth commandment teach us?

A. The sixth commandment teaches us that we should never take away someone's life unlawfully.

Q13. What is the seventh commandment?

A. The seventh commandment is: *You shall not commit adultery.*

Q14. What does the seventh commandment teach us?

A. The seventh commandment teaches us that marriage must be kept pure and only between a husband and wife.

Q15. What is the eighth commandment?

A. The eighth commandment is: *You shall not steal.*

Q16. What does the eighth commandment teach us?

A. The eighth commandment teaches us that we should never take away things that rightfully belong to other people.

Q17. What is the ninth commandment?

A. The ninth commandment is: *You shall not bear false witness against your neighbor.*

Q18. What does the ninth commandment teach us?

A. The ninth commandment teaches us to be truthful, especially in things we say about other people.

Q19. What is the tenth commandment?

A. The tenth commandment is: *You shall not covet.*

Q20. What does the tenth commandment teach us?

A. The tenth commandment teaches us to be content with what we have.

Catechism on the Tabernacle & Feasts

Q1. What was the Tabernacle?

    A. The Tabernacle was a large tent used by the Israelites as a place of worship.

Q2. Which two things were in the courtyard of the Tabernacle?

    A. The altar and the basin were in the courtyard.

Q3. Which three things were in the Holy Place in the Tabernacle?

    A. The golden candlestick, table of showbread, and altar of incense were in the Holy Place.

Q4. What was in the Most Holy Place?

    A. The Ark of the Covenant was in the Most Holy Place.

Q5. What was inside the Ark of the Covenant?

    A. Aaron's rod, a jar of manna, and the tablets containing the Ten Commandments.

Q6. Which feasts did God instruct the Israelites to celebrate?

    A. There were seven feasts: Passover, Unleavened Bread, First Fruits, Pentecost, Trumpets, Atonement, and Tabernacles.

Types of Law Chart

Give me understanding, and I shall keep Your law;
Indeed, I shall observe it with my whole heart. – Psalm 119:34

TYPE OF LAW	DEFINITION	EXAMPLE
MORAL	Laws pertaining to moral righteousness, summarized in the Ten Commandments	You shall love the LORD your God with all your heart, with all your soul, and with all your strength. – Deut. 6:5 You shall not steal. – Exodus 20:15
CEREMONIAL	Laws instructing Israel regarding worship (sacrifices, feasts, the Tabernacle)	You shall keep the Feast of Unleavened Bread. – Exodus 23:15 And you shall offer your burnt offerings, the meat and the blood, on the altar of the LORD your God. – Deut. 12:27
JUDICIAL (CIVIL)	Laws giving guidelines on community life (public safety, inheritance, property division)	When you build a new house, then you shall make a parapet for your roof, that you may not bring guilt of bloodshed on your household if anyone falls from it. – Deut. 22:8

Ten Commandments Chart

And God spoke all these words, saying,
"I am the LORD your God, who brought you out of the land of Egypt,
out of the house of bondage."
– Exodus 20:1-2

SUMMARY	FULL TEXT (Exodus 20)
Do not worship other gods.	You shall have no other gods before Me.
Do not make idols.	You shall not make for yourself a carved image – any likeness of anything that is in heaven above or that is in the earth beneath, or that is in the water under the earth; you shall not bow down to them nor serve them. For I, the LORD your God, am a jealous God, visiting the iniquity of the fathers upon the children to the third and fourth generations of those who hate Me, but showing mercy to thousands, to those who love Me and keep My commandments.
Do not misuse God's name.	You shall not take the name of the LORD your God in vain, for the LORD will not hold him guiltless who takes His name in vain.
Keep the Sabbath day holy.	Remember the Sabbath day, to keep it holy. Six days you shall labor and do all your work, but the seventh day is the Sabbath of the LORD your God. In it you shall do no work: you, nor your son, nor your daughter, nor your male servant, nor your female servant, nor your cattle, nor your stranger who is within your gates. For in six days the LORD made the heavens and the earth, the sea, and all that is in them, and rested on the seventh day. Therefore, the LORD blessed the Sabbath day and hallowed it.
Honor your parents.	Honor your father and your mother, that your days may be long upon the land which the LORD your God is giving you.

Do not murder.	You shall not murder.
Do not commit adultery.	You shall not commit adultery.
Do not steal.	You shall not steal.
Do not give false testimony.	You shall not bear false witness against your neighbor.
Do not be envious.	You shall not covet your neighbor's house; you shall not covet your neighbor's wife, nor his male servant, nor his female servant, nor his ox, nor his donkey, nor anything that is your neighbor's.

Feasts Chart

You shall have a song
As in the night when a holy festival is kept,
And gladness of heart as when one goes with a flute,
To come into the mountain of the LORD,
To the Mighty One of Israel.
– Isaiah 30:29

FEAST	How was it celebrated?
PASSOVER	Eating a lamb with bitter herbs and bread without yeast. This feast commemorated the day that God delivered the Israelites from slavery in Egypt.
UNLEAVENED BREAD	Offerings, assemblies, and eating bread made without yeast. This feast was a continuation of the Passover celebration.
FIRST FRUITS	Offering the first barley harvest to the Lord.
PENTECOST	Offering the wheat harvest to the Lord.
TRUMPETS	A day of assembly called with trumpet blasts.
ATONEMENT	A day of fasting and sacrifices for sin.
TABERNACLES	Living in shelters for a week and celebrating the fruit harvest.

Rhyme on the Law

Love the Lord;
Obey His Word;
Remember the commands you heard;
Idol worship is absurd!
This is the law of God.

Sabbath is
A day of rest,
Trust the Lord; He knows what's best.
If you obey, you will be blessed.
This is the law of God.

Don't be cruel;
Just do what's right;
Consider well the poor man's plight;
Don't keep his garments overnight.
This is the law of God.

You're in court
To testify -
Don't take a bribe; don't tell a lie;
God hears the righteous when they cry.
This is the law of God.

If you steal
You must repay;
If you vow, then don't delay;
Speak God's name? Watch what you say!
This is the law of God.

The Tabernacle

There is a river whose streams shall make glad the city of God,
The holy place of the tabernacle of the Most High. – Psalm 46:4

The Tabernacle was a place of worship for the Israelites built during their journey through the desert on the way to the Promised Land. It was constructed of materials that could be easily moved from place to place because the Israelites did not yet have a permanent home. Whenever they moved to a new place, the priests would take the Tabernacle down and carry it to the next camp.

The Tabernacle had a courtyard surrounded by linen curtains held up by posts. The altar for burnt offerings was within this courtyard. Near the altar stood a basin for the priests to wash themselves before entering the tent of the Tabernacle.

Inside the tent, the priests came first to an outer area called the Holy Place containing the golden candlestick, the table of showbread, and the altar of incense. At the back of the Tabernacle was an interior room hidden behind a curtain. This was the Most Holy Place, and it housed the Ark of the Covenant.

DIAGRAM OF THE TABERNACLE

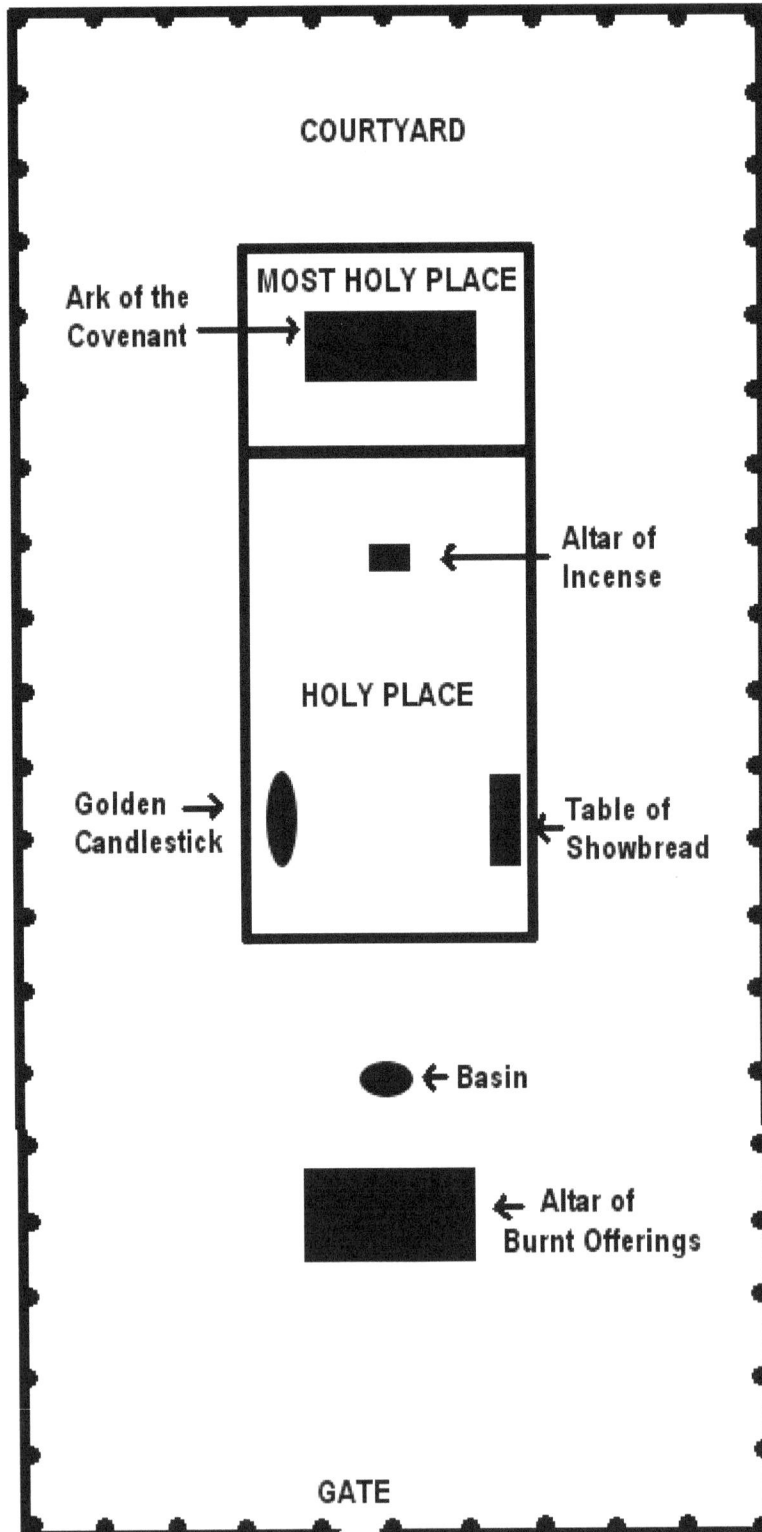

COURTYARD

MOST HOLY PLACE

Ark of the
Covenant

Altar of
Incense

HOLY PLACE

Golden
Candlestick

Table of
Showbread

Basin

Altar of
Burnt Offerings

GATE

The Ark of the Covenant

Then the priests brought the ark of the covenant of the LORD to its place, into the inner sanctuary of the temple, to the Most Holy Place, under the wings of the cherubim. – I Kings 8:6

The **Ark of the Covenant** was a large box constructed of acacia wood and covered with a layer of gold. The Ark was carried by poles inserted through rings on both sides. On the top of the Ark was a lid called the **Mercy Seat**. Two golden cherubim (angels) stood on the ends of the Mercy Seat. Inside the ark were placed the stone tablets containing the Ten Commandments, a jar of manna, and Aaron's rod.

The Ark of the Covenant was kept in the Most Holy Place in the Tabernacle. Only specially appointed Levites were permitted to carry the Ark.

The Ark Passes Over the Jordan
Painting by James Jacque Joseph Tissot, c.1900